Essential Communications Skills for Managers

Essential Communications Skills for Managers, Volume I

A Practical Guide for Communicating Effectively with All People in All Situations

Walter St. John
Ben Haskell

BEP BUSINESS EXPERT PRESS

Essential Communications Skills for Managers, Volume I: A Practical Guide for Communicating Effectively with All People in All Situations
Copyright © Business Expert Press, LLC, 2017.

First published in 2017 by
Business Expert Press, LLC
222 East 46th Street, New York, NY 10017
www.businessexpertpress.com

ISBN-13: 978-1-63157-654-6 (paperback)
ISBN-13: 978-1-63157-655-3 (e-book)

Business Expert Press Corporate Communication Collection

Collection ISSN: 2156-8162 (print)
Collection ISSN: 2156-8170 (electronic)

Cover and interior design by S4Carlisle Publishing Services
Private Ltd., Chennai, India

First edition: 2017

10 9 8 7 6 5 4 3 2 1

Printed in the United States of America.

Dedication

*We dedicate this book to all the managers
who are committed to achieving excellence,
at all times, when communicating
with people on the job.*

Abstract

The purpose of this book is to provide practicing and aspiring managers and students of management a practical and comprehensive reference source for communicating on the job with all people in all situations. This "how-to" book provides readers with the essential knowledge, attitudes, and skills to perform the communicating aspects of their routine and special duties. The information is presented in two volumes. Each topic is divided into "Things to Know" and "Things to Do."

The topics are divided into six sections:

- Overview of the Book
- Fundamentals of Communicating
- Communicating Competencies Required of Managers
- Personal Qualities Managers Need to Communicate Effectively
- Communicating Strategies for Safeguarding the Manager's Job
- Communicating Effectively in Stressful Situations

Keywords

Communicating Effectively, Communicating for Managers, Communicating in a Crisis, Communicating in the Workplace, Communicating with Employees, Communication, Communicating Strategies, Communicating under Stress, Communication Effectiveness for Managers, Communication Fundamentals, Communication Guide for Managers, Communication Mistakes, Communication Reference Guide for Managers, Communication Skills, Conflict Resolution, Diversity Communication, Gender-Neutral, Listening Tips, Managerial Performance, Management Skills, Managerial Communications, Persuasive Communication, Reading Tips, Speaking Confidently, Speechmaking, Workplace Communications, Workplace Situations, Writing Tips

Contents

Acknowledgments

Our sincere thanks to those who helped with this book along the way.

Typist Janice Gromm
University of Maine Reference Library
Husson University Reference Library
Interviews with six experienced and successful managers
The writings of authorities on communication and management
Friends, associates, and professional colleagues

SECTION 1

TOPIC 1

Overview of the Book

Communication is:

- The lifeblood of all organizations
- Of great importance to all managers
- Involved in every thought and action by managers
- The difference between success and failure of managers today
- A managerial imperative

The purpose of this book is to provide readers with a comprehensive reference source for communicating with all kinds of people, in all kinds of situations in the workplace.

This book is designed for practicing managers, new managers, and as a college textbook, for students studying management and communications. It provides managers with the essential knowledge, attitudes, and skills to perform their responsibilities competently.

The 43 topics plus Overview and Index of this "How To" book are practical instead of theoretical, specific instead of general, and offer realistic information about successfully communicating in the workplace.

As a convenience to readers, topics are listed in a detailed Table of Contents. The book is organized into two volumes with six and five sections respectively so that the reader can expeditiously find information of special interest. The reader's time is saved by the use of bullet lists to present the topics in a concise manner. Each topic is presented in two categories: (1) Things to Know and (2) Things to Do.

The writing style is informal and reader friendly. The information is presented in a straightforward, direct to the point, no-nonsense manner. Plain and simple English is used rather than technical or scholarly language. Common sense and practicality are emphasized and theory de-emphasized. Each topic is complete in itself and can be read in only a few minutes.

Readers of professional books are typically interested in learning about the author's qualifications for writing on the subject. Therefore, let's take a moment to provide the authors' training and experience in management and communications. Both authors:

- Have served as managers in both the private and public sectors
- Have taught management and communications courses at the college/university level for many years
- Have served as officers in the U.S. Army
- Have had a lifelong interest in communications
- Made numerous presentations to prestigious groups

Dr. Walter St. John is a semiretired writer who is married and lives on the outskirts of Bangor, Maine. His public sector experience was as an educational administrator, coach, and counselor. His private sector experience was in Human Resource Management with the Hershey Foods Corporation and Director of Management for a national trade association.

Dr. St. John served as a state university administrator and professor of management and communications courses. He is the author of numerous books and articles, including the communications section of *The Encyclopedia of School Administration and Supervision*. He has presented communications programs for organizations such as The American Management Association. Dr. St. John's training in management and communications includes a Bachelor's Degree with a major in Speech Communication from the University of Arizona. He earned his Doctoral Degree from the University of Southern California with a major in Management and a Minor in Counseling.

Ben Haskell is married, the father of two grown daughters, has four grandsons, and lives in Brewer, Maine. He retired in 2014 after serving for twenty-six years as Executive Vice-President and Academic Dean of the New England School of Communications of Husson University in Bangor, Maine.

After finishing college, Ben served as an officer in the U.S. Army with duty in Vietnam where he served as an advisor to the ARVN Military

Police. He began his professional career in Maine where he was employed as staff announcer and later as Program Director of two radio stations in the City of Ellsworth.

In 1988 Ben accepted the position of Director of The New England School of Broadcasting in Bangor, Maine where he also taught Radio Announcing and Production courses. The school changed its name to the New England School of Communications in the late 1990s and remained an independent school on campus until 2014 when it officially merged with Husson University.

In his 26 years of serving higher education students, Ben was instrumental in helping the school grow from a one-year certificate program with 30 students, to a four-year degree-granting institution offering three Bachelor of Science degrees in eight different areas of study and with a peak enrollment of 520 students. Although retired, Ben continues to teach select Communications courses at the school. Most recently, he was honored with induction into the Maine Association of Broadcasters Hall of Fame for 2015.

His undergraduate training was at the University of Maine where he received a BA Degree in Speech Communications with a concentration in radio/TV and theater. He earned his Master's Degree in Business from Husson University.

His current activities include sailing, gardening, reading, writing, and becoming a Maine/Florida "Snowbird." He is active in his church at the state and local levels, and continues to serve on the Boards of Directors of the United Way of Eastern Maine and the BTS Center (formerly Bangor Theological Seminary).

SECTION 2

TOPIC 2

Fundamentals of Communicating

"It is difficult to imagine any aspect of executive work
that does not involve communicating or relating to others"
—Robert Wilson

A. Things to Know

1. Definition of Communication:

- It is the process of passing information and understanding from one person to another person
- An essential part of any correct definition makes it clear that it is a two-way interaction between two or more people

2. Goals of Communicating:

- To convey information and share knowledge
- To increase understanding
- To influence thinking
- To gain acceptance for what is said
- To encourage action

3. Importance of Communication:

- Communicating is the most significant ingredient in any kind of management. Studies indicate that approximately 70 percent of a manager's work day is devoted to communicating with people.
- The challenge of achieving and maintaining effective communication in an organization is increasingly awesome because the need is great and the barriers many.

- As organizations increase in size and complexity, the amount of communication increases as do the related communication problems (thus more time is needed to deal with them).

4. Key Components of the Communicating Process:

To communicate successfully, managers need to understand the seven components of the communications process. These essential elements are:

1. Sender—from whom
2. Receiver—to whom
3. Message—the what
4. Medium/method—how
5. Channel—where
6. Timing—when
7. Feedback—response

In addition, every communication occurs within an existing climate or situation that influences the receiver's attitude and reaction to the message.

5. Facts about the Components/Elements:

1. The sender perceives a need to communicate and identifies the specific purpose. The sender next clarifies his/her thinking because no one can communicate anything clearly to anyone else that isn't first clear in his/her own mind. The sender then selects the receivers for the message.
2. The receiver needs to strive to be receptive to all messages sent to him/her and to view them objectively and with an open mind. Also, the receiver should give 100 percent attention to the message to understand it.
3. The message is the content or subject of a communication.
   A message can contain one or more of the following: facts, ideas, feelings, opinions, and perceptions. A message can include both implicit and explicit information. It is imperative that the receiver understands the message as intended by the sender.
4. The medium is the method, way, or technique used to send a message. The message's purpose, the receivers, and the message content determine the best medium to use. There are two types of media:

formal (for example, a letter) and informal (for example, a hand-written note).

- In addition, there are three methods used to communicate a message: (1) verbal (by words), (2) nonverbal (by voice tone), and (3) by body language through facial expressions or gestures.
- It is essential that your words, voice tone, and body language be consistent with each other and that they all send the same message or the person listening will receive a mixed message and become confused about the real message being conveyed.

5. Channels of Communication
   - Communications channels are the routes, levels, and networks that messages flow through to reach their receivers.
   - Organizations use both official (formal) channels and unofficial (informal) channels (for example, the grapevine) to disseminate information throughout the organization.
   - Information flows in three directions or routes: (1) upward from subordinates to superiors; (2) downward from superiors to subordinates; and (3) horizontally (laterally) among employees occupying equally important positions.
   - Flatter channels (fewer levels) are preferable because the information flows faster, encourages a more accurate exchange of information (because of less filtering), and consequently there is less misunderstanding and fewer circulations of rumors.
   - Downward flow of information is the fastest and the most reliable. They set activities in motion, prepare employees for changes, and explain policies and procedures.
   - Upward communications are slower and less reliable than downward communications.
   - Horizontal communications are used to keep peers informed and to coordinate people and activities. Lateral communications are typically used infrequently or neglected entirely in many organizations.

6. Timing of Messages
   - The timing of a message is crucial. It involves such factors as: (1) frequency of messages, (2) spacing of messages, (3) situation when sent and received (for example, during a peak work time,

and (4) the immediately preceding or following important events (such as layoffs).

- The timing of messages is determined by the message content, the location of the target groups, speed of the channels, and the urgency of the situation.

7. Feedback to Messages
   - Feedback is an integral part of the communications process but is typically neglected. Effective feedback calls for the receivers to respond or verify that they received and understood the message.
   - Verbal communication provides better opportunities for feedback than written methods because it allows for instant clarification and the observation of body language cues by both sender and receiver.

6. Methods of Communicating

There are four distinct methods for communicating: (1) speaking, (2) listening, (3) reading, and (4) writing.

- It is imperative that managers become skilled in the use of each of these skills because they are so important. Most managers listen the most, speak the second most followed by reading and lastly writing when communicating on the job.
- It is important to be aware that a person cannot not communicate. People communicate all of the time regardless of whether they intend to or not. (Please note that each of the four communicating methods is discussed in detail later in the book.)

7. Important Misconceptions about Communicating

- Managers need to become aware of and avoid having these common misconceptions in order to communicate effectively:
   1. Believing that effective communication just happens effortlessly
   2. Assuming that when one speaks or writes he/she automatically communicates
   3. Thinking that effective communication can be only one way
   4. Equating communicating with understanding and understanding with acceptance of the message
   5. Expecting all of the organizations communications to follow official channels

6. Believing that communications channels and chain of command are identical
7. Emphasizing the sending of a message rather than the receiving of the message
8. Assuming that close and frequent contact guarantees good communication
9. Considering communication to be primarily a matter of technique and more important than attitude
10. Expecting to be able to communicate meaning exactly
11. Failing to recognize the importance of feedback and climate
12. Assuming that people view events, reality, and facts the same way
13. Believing that meaning is in words rather than in people
14. Thinking that facts should always be emphasized and feelings deemphasized
15. Concentrating on what you are going to say because you consider it to be much more important than how you are going to say it
16. Assuming that all people think the same as you do and that all words have the same meaning to all people
17. Believing that if you communicate clearly that there is no need to secure feedback to verify that you have been understood
18. Assuming that if people are looking at you attentively that they are actually listening to you
19. Believing that the message you are sending is the message being heard
20. Considering that it is more important to get understood by people than to understand what people are saying to you

8. Barriers to Effective Communicating

- Managers need to be aware of the numerous barriers that interfere with communicating successfully so they can avoid as many of them as possible
- These categories of communication barriers are straightforward and should help managers to keep them in mind when communicating
- There are four types of barriers: (1) interpersonal, (2) structural/procedural, (3) situational/timing, and (4) language

Interpersonal Barriers:

1. Interpersonal

   - Status, role, and job differences
   - Lifestyle and experience differences
   - Age and sex differences
   - Differences in people: education, intelligence, and ability to think
   - Preconceived ideas and beliefs
   - Unique perceptions and ways of filtering information that distorts meaning
   - People preoccupied with own activities and interests
   - Personality conflicts between senders and receivers
   - Apathy and lack of desire to relate and cooperate
   - Fear of new ideas and resistance to change
   - People inclined to listen to refute what they hear rather than to understand it
   - Closed mindedness and stereotyping of people's racial, ethnic, religious, and cultural differences
   - Disregard of people's feelings and emphasis on facts and events and situations
   - Penalizing of people for new ideas and nonconformity

2. Structural and Procedural Barriers:

   - Too many levels in channels of communication
   - Channels too busy and too slow
   - Horizontal communication inadequate
   - Overemphasis on downward and underemphasis on upward communicating
   - Overreliance on official channels of communication
   - Spatial distance and infrequent incidental contact between managers and subordinates
   - Organization too big and inflexible
   - Overreliance on one-way and written communications
   - Fear of admitting mistakes and problems
   - The proper method for transmitting specific kinds of information is often unknown.

3. Situational and Timing Barriers:
   - People too busy or rushed to pay adequate attention when sending and receiving frequent messages (for example, e-mails)
   - Important information delayed or not received at all
   - Suspicious or hostile climate exists
   - Too much noise and confusion interferes with the ability to concentrate on understanding messages
   - Lack of privacy for having important or confidential discussions
   - Uncomfortable facilities for prolonged discussions
   - Too many distractions and too much competition for close attention to communicating
   - Timing is wrong and affects receptivity to the message
   - Information overload

4. Language Barriers:
   - Multiple meanings for words
   - Inexact and changing meaning of words
   - Technical terms, specialized language, and unfamiliar words
   - Unclear thought and vague expression of thoughts
   - Inadequate vocabulary and incorrect or imprecise use of words
   - Inflammatory or abusive word choice creating negative feelings within receivers of such messages
   - Too many words used in one message
   - Disorganized or illogical stating of ideas
   - People assuming words have only one meaning—theirs
   - Indefinite and nonspecific language use
   - Diverse workforce often has limited understanding of the English language
   - Messages lack brevity—they tend to be wordy and ramble
   - Sloppy articulation and incorrect pronunciation of words
   - Use of generalizations and abstract terms without accompanying explanations

TOPIC 3

Important Principles for Sending and Receiving Communications

"Important Principles May and Must be Inflexible"
—Abraham Lincoln

A. Things to Know

1. Principles for Senders to Observe:

These principles for sending communications should help you to be an effective communicator:

- Sending too much information too frequently can be almost as big a problem as sending too little information too infrequently
- Meaning is in people, not in the words themselves
- Realize and accept the fact that it is the sender's primary responsibility to get the message understood
- Know your purpose, think, and identify your receivers before sending a message
- Identify the key communicators in your organization and keep them appropriately informed
- Have the courage to level with people but balance your leveling with tact and consideration for the person's feelings
- Exhibit proper attitude when communicating and receiving communications and recognize that your attitude is more important than your communicating technique
- Realize that all communications are filtered and consequently at least some of your message will be distorted and thus misunderstood
- Understand and accept that your image influences how people respond to your communications—as the saying goes, "how can I hear what you are saying when there is so much of you saying it"

B. Things to Do

- Seek to understand people as hard as you seek to get understood by them
- Treat people as they want to be treated—not as you want to be treated (all people are different)
- Personalize your messages and use familiar language and words—make them compatible with the receiver's interests, intelligence, education, and experience
- Stress you, we, and our when communicating and play down I, me, and my
- Minimize status and social distance when communicating with your subordinates—treat them as adults and people with value
- Follow up on employee requests and your promises—remember to address "the little things"
- Say what you mean, mean what you say, and show that you mean it
- Be explicit—say what you mean as precisely as possible
- Promote understanding by telling people what you are going to tell them, telling them what you want to tell them, and telling them what you have told them
- Communicate effectively by talking to the right people, in the right way, at the right time and at the right place
- Keep employees well informed and give them advance notice on all important matters
- Explain the reasons for your decisions and actions unless they involve confidential matters
- Seek feedback to verify that your message was received, understood, and to obtain receiver's reactions
- Increase the size of your vocabulary by diligently looking up new words and using them periodically
- Share important, detailed, and complete information face-to-face to permit instant feedback
- Use an appropriate voice tone when talking to people; avoid sounding abrasive, superior, or condescending to people
- State the purpose of your communication early and clearly to gain your receiver's attention

- When communicating talk less and listen more
- Be sincere, candid, and straightforward when communicating to create trust and credibility
- Inform employees about things before informing the public

2. Principles for Receivers to Observe

A. Things to Know

- Receivers are expected to keep an open mind and to listen to understand, not to refute what is being said to them
- Receivers are responsible for asking questions to seek clarification on matters they don't understand
- Receivers are expected to pay close attention to what is being said to them and to avoid getting distracted
- Receivers should pay more attention to what a person is saying to them rather than concentrating on who is saying it
- Receivers should pay strict attention to what the person speaking is saying rather than concentrating on what they want to say next
- Receivers need to refrain from interrupting a speaker's comments unless they need to clarify a point being made by the person talking

B. Things to Do

- Demonstrate an interest in what the person talking is saying
- Free up your mind so you can concentrate on what you are hearing rather than being preoccupied with your own thoughts
- Figure out how the information you are hearing can be helpful to you
- Listen to the main points rather than getting lost in the details of the message being delivered
- Repeat the main ideas mentally to make sure you understand them
- Distinguish between facts, opinions, perceptions, ideas, and inferences

Please note that more information on how to receive and use information most effectively is offered in the listening tips presented later in this book.

TOPIC 4

Communications Rights of Employees

"Employees are entitled to prompt and honest answers to their questions, suggestions, and requests"

—unknown

A. Things to Know

Specific communications rights of employees include:

Receiving an immediate and comprehensive orientation regarding the organization, their work unit, and their job including the following information:

1. The organization's mission, philosophy, traditions, and culture
2. Organization's structure, policies, and procedures
3. Organization's expectations re: employee conduct and performance
4. Organization's compensation and benefits package
5. Organization's annual goals, priorities, and plans
6. Individual employee's specific job authority, responsibilities, goals, and priorities
7. Individual employee's freedom and constraints re: doing his/her job as well as the resources and assistance available for performing the job
8. Receiving a copy of the Employee's Handbook including a chart showing the chain of command and the channels and procedures for communicating
9. Receiving communications training consistent with the organization's expectations and with his/her job responsibilities
10. Be communicated with regularly about important matters rather than only sporadically and in times of crisis
11. Communicated on a right to know basis rather than on a need to know basis

12. Be kept promptly and fully informed on all vital matters affecting the organization, their work unit, and their job

13. Have ready access to their supervisor to discuss job-related matters, especially problems

14. Be leveled with re: expected performance, current performance, important changes, promotional prospects, and organization's accomplishments and problems

15. Receive clear messages stated in simple and understandable language

16. Be communicated with in a "socially" acceptable manner and as an adult with dignity as a person

17. Have bad news (problems) shared candidly as well as good news (achievements) and be given reasons for proposed changes as well as decisions and actions routinely whenever they affect their own work

18. Have all important or sensitive matters discussed face-to-face whenever possible

19. Be provided an opportunity to express themselves freely, in an appropriate manner, re: all important matters pertaining to their job

20. Be listened to, heard, and receive an appropriate response

21. Have an opportunity to make constructive criticisms, offer suggestions, and share ideas freely on all appropriate matters without recrimination

22. Have an opportunity to provide both input and feedback on all important matters affecting their work before the decisions are made and actions occur

23. Have all confidential information contained in their personnel file protected and confidences honored

24. Have an up-to-date job description with an opportunity for input before it is adopted

25. Have input into their annual performance goals and priorities as well as their performance evaluation

TOPIC 5

Communications Responsibilities of Employees

"To be a Man is, precisely to be responsible"
—Antonie Desaint - Exupery

A. Things to Know

Employees have not only communications rights, but responsibilities. These are some of the most important ones:

- To view communicating as an ongoing and essential job function and to conduct oneself in a manner consistent with this viewpoint
- To seek and receive necessary communications training commensurate with the organization's communications expectations, and one's job responsibilities
- To consistently practice recommended communications principles and techniques
- To have a positive attitude toward one's communication responsibilities and enthusiastically promote a healthy communications climate
- To actively seek information needed to do one's job well
- To share appropriate information readily and promptly (both proactively and upon request)
- To provide information (both input and feedback) whenever it serves the best interests of the organization and its employees
- To share the right information with the right people at the right time in the right way
- To speak up, in a straightforward manner, on all important matters concerning the welfare of the organization and work unit

- To level with coworkers without damaging their self-esteem and creating resentment
- To use the receiver's preferred method for receiving messages as much as is practical
- To communicate clearly in a sincere, straightforward, and ethical manner
- To follow all communications-related policies and procedures
- To avoid over-communicating and sending unnecessary information
- To strive to have, and to show, interest in the other person's viewpoint and to listen with an open receptive mind
- To give people the information they want and need when they need and want it
- To faithfully observe approved channels for communicating, except for emergencies
- To be ethical by keeping one's superior fully informed of problems and deviations from the action plan
- To strive to get understood and to understand by seeking verification through feedback
- To demonstrate a respect for the other person's time by being as brief as possible when communicating
- To protect confidential information and honor confidences
- To be candid with managers rather than playing it safe by telling them only what you think they want to hear

TOPIC 6

Communications Responsibilities of Managers

"Managers are responsible for implementing the organization's communications
policies and providing employees the necessary information to
perform their duties effectively"

—unknown

A. Things to Know

Managers have definite communications responsibilities that they are expected to meet. Some of the main one's are:

- To help plan the organization's communications philosophy, goals, policies, and procedures
- To implement the goals, policies, and procedures
- To identify communications needs and problems within their work unit as well as organization wide
- To keep lines of communication open between management and employees
- To provide employees support and resources to meet the organization's communications goals and carry out its policies
- Things to Do:
- To develop and follow procedures for implementing policies:
  1. To encourage by words and actions the creating and maintaining of a healthy communications climate
  2. To disseminate information to employees through official channels
  3. To train or secure training for employees re: the basics of communicating
  4. To identify key positions in the organization that he/she needs to keep informed regularly
  5. Keep up to date on the latest developments in the field of communications
  6. To evaluate the appropriate supervisors and employees re: their communications strengths and weaknesses and develop a plan for them to improve their performance as needed

Suggested Communications Training for Managers

"Responsible managers receive the appropriate type and amount of communications training"
—unknown

A. Things to Know and B. Things To Do

- The goal of managerial training in communications is to provide all levels of management with the basic knowledge and skills required to be effective managers
- Much of the communications training of managers can be conducted on-site and coordinated by the training department of the organization and conducted by a communications specialist
- There are a wide variety of training opportunities available to interested managers. These include:
  1. On-site group training
  2. Completion of college home studies or correspondence communications courses
  3. Tailored communications reading programs recommended by communications consultants
  4. Watching select videos dealing with communication
  5. Attendance at off-site communications workshops presented by communications specialists
  6. Participating in off-site community college or university courses (regular classes or computer based)
  7. Listening to tapes on communication while commuting, traveling, or at home
- High priority communications training should include these essential subjects:
  1. Fundamentals of communicating
  2. Speaking/presentation skills

3. Listening/responding skills
4. Communicating with a diverse workforce
5. Use of sex-neutral/fair language
6. Handling job-related conflict and employee complaints
7. New communications technology available
8. Reading and writing skills, time permitting

- Manager's efforts to improve their communications knowledge and skills should be recognized and rewarded by the organization.
- A manager's ability to communicate effectively should be rated annually as an important part of the manager's performance reviews and evaluation.

SECTION 3

TOPIC 8

Communicating Competencies Required By Managers

"There is no indispensable Man"
—Theodore Roosevelt

A. Things to Know

- Managers need to have numerous communications competencies to succeed
- The required competencies continue to grow. For example: How to communicate with a diverse workforce, how to use gender fair language, how to avoid saying things that constitute sexual harassment, and how to use the new technology
- The following list includes most of the communication knowledge and skills that today's managers need to communicate effectively with individuals and groups on-the-job:
  1. Being both accessible and approachable
  2. Knowing, understanding, and adhering to legal requirements, organizational policies, and provisions of the union contract
  3. Being aware of and practicing recommended communications practices
  4. Understanding the key elements of an effective communication
  5. Possessing the ability to size up people and communicate with the most difficult kinds of coworkers
  6. Having the ability to understand and to get understood

7. Sending the right people the right message in the right way at the right time
8. Using the best methods for communicating with different kinds of people
9. Knowing how to conserve time when interacting with people without sounding abrupt or being abrasive
10. Being able to speak and write clearly, simply, concisely, and directly to the point
11. Knowing when it is better to talk or better to listen
12. Realizing the times when it is best to remain silent and knowing the ways for being noncommittal without offending people

B. Things to Do

- Create and maintain positive relationships with people and a healthy communications climate
- Putting people at ease and being comfortable when engaged in small talk
- Asking questions effectively to draw people out in order to secure information
- Securing feedback to show you understand or to gain additional information. Protecting confidences and confidential information
- Using and observing body language skillfully
- Planning and conducting productive meetings
- Contributing to meetings as a participant
- Communicating calmly and patiently in stressful situations
- Negotiating skillfully
- Disagreeing agreeably
- Using effective communications techniques and mediating conflicts
- Having the persuasive skills needed to overcome people's objections to your ideas and proposals
- Following recommended methods for speaking, listening, writing, and reading
- Using a flexible communicating style in order to adapt to other people's communicating style

- Developing and using an extensive vocabulary so you can select the most precise words when saying something important
- Skimming information being read to save time
- Listening compassionately to the person speaking and objectively to what he/she is saying
- Listening patiently, attentively, and perceptively to the facts and feelings being expressed by employees
- Identifying the main points versus the details when listening or reading

TOPIC 9

The Manager's Availability for Communicating

"Availability has two equally important dimensions – accessibility and approachability"

—Walter StJohn

A. Things to Know

- One of an organization's most serious and pervasive problems is the unavailability of managers to communicate with employees when needed
- There are two dimensions of availability: (1) accessibility and (2) approachability
- Accessibility involves physical presence. It is vital that managers be perceived as "being there" for employees when needed.
- Approachability involves a manager's mental receptivity to communicate with employees. The manager's words and body language need to convey that the manager sincerely wants to talk with employees and welcomes the opportunity to do so.
- Ideally a manager should be both accessible and approachable to communicate with employees when they need to talk with him/her. However, the fact is that it is impossible for managers to always be available to their employees.
- These suggestions will help managers to use their time to best advantage and result in their being more available to their employees:

1. Avoid unnecessary interruptions such as: low priority phone calls, non-stop e-mails, drop by "visitors" who typically begin their comments with "are you busy?" or "got a minute?"
2. When interrupted managers need to ask themselves "Is this important enough for me to stop doing what I am doing now?" If it isn't

sufficiently important don't permit the interruption but inform the employee when you will be available to meet with him or her.

3. Managers need to ask colleagues in a polite manner to stop routinely sending them copies of e-mails, memos, letters, and other unnecessary communications.

- Managers need to request that their office assistant screen phone calls, visitors, and to discard unimportant mail
- Managers need a "please do not disturb sign" on their office door at the same time every day and ask employees to honor the request except for emergencies (unfortunately managers soon learn that the word emergency has many interpretations and that their request is unrealistic)
- Managers need to have the final say on all tentative appointments made by the office assistant
- Managers who report to work an hour before their employees, and or, stay an hour after the employees have left work can get loads of work done without fear of interruptions
- Managers who leave their office and quickly "make the rounds" can productively take care of new business at their convenience rather than having employees see them in their office at inopportune times
- Let's take a closer look at both accessibility and approachability
- Managers can demonstrate their accessibility by:
  1. Being easy to see and talk to
  2. Allowing employees to talk to them without going through an intermediary or always having to make an appointment
  3. Maintaining an open door policy with the door swinging both in and out
  4. Wandering around the work areas and interacting with employees in the various departments
- Managers can show they are approachable by:
  1. Seeing employees who want to see them quickly
  2. Paying full attention to what the employee is saying rather than acting preoccupied with their own concerns and problems

3. Allowing no interruptions when conversing with an employee

4. Giving employees the time they need without acting rushed

5. Listening attentively and asking questions related to what the employee has been saying

6. Being open-minded and receptive to an employee's suggestions

B. Things to Do

- The management by wandering around technique (MBWA) shows that managers are both accessible and approachable
- MBWA has great potential, so let's examine the concept in greater detail
- The essence of the idea is that managers regularly leave their office to go out to the employees' work areas instead of expecting employees to come to their office
- This communications approach is more comfortable for employees because the conversations occur on their home turf
- These suggestions will help managers succeed with the MBWA technique:
  1. Walk around slowly in a relaxed manner, pause frequently to say hi to people and engage in small talk
- Ask employees simple questions such as "How's it going?" or "is there anything you would like to talk with me about?" Wait after you ask the question and act as though you want and expect an answer
- Avoid acting too businesslike when strolling aroundDon't act as though you were conducting an inspection
- Look relaxed and approachable by taking off your coat and loosening your tie and rolling up your sleeves
- Take different routes when walking to and from the parking lot, the cafeteria, restrooms, and fitness center
- Drop by department meetings occasionally to say hello and to receive some feedback on a subject of interest—but don't stay too long or you will disrupt the meeting
- Visit all departments and work shifts at different times both day and night. Try to vary your "drop by" times and visiting

pattern so your visit will not look planned (be sure not to overlook any departments or work areas)

- Show that you know what is going on in the departments and that you know things about the employees and their work (use the employee's names when you know them and be sure to pronounce them correctly)
- Get a feel for the different departments by working in them periodically for a day or two (get your hands dirty and mix "with the troops")
- Eat at different times and places with employees but before sitting down ask people if you may join them as a courtesy
- Stand at different traffic centers in the facility at the start and end of special days so you can greet the employees and wish them well (this action is especially important on major holidays as it gives you an opportunity to wish employees a merry Christmas, etc.)
- Go to different water fountains, coffeemakers, restrooms, and duplicating areas to "bump" into employees you seldom see
- Attend the organization's social events and mix informally with the employees and their families
- Ride with coworkers to off-site meetings and conferences
- Exercise at noon or after work at the organization's fitness center (by doing this you also show support for the fitness program)
- Establish communication councils and quality circles and meet with them regularly away from your office
- Invite other managers and supervisors to have lunch with you on occasion

TOPIC 10

Sizing Up Coworkers Accurately

"Things are not always as they seem"

—Phacdrus

A. Things to Know and Things to Do

- When you size up a person you form an opinion or make a judgment about the person. You try to figure out what makes the person tick
- The more quickly and accurately you are able to size up the person you are communicating with the better
- It is essential that you are aware of, and factor in, your prejudices toward people if your sizing up method is to be valid and reliable
- Sizing up people has three dimensions:
  1. What to size up about the person
  2. How to size up the person
  3. When to sizes up the individual
- Before you can accurately size up someone you need to know exactly what to look for

Things to look for:
  1. Person's personality and attitude
  2. Person's thought process
  3. Person's knowledge and ability to understand
  4. Person's communicating style
     - Let's begin with examining the attitude of the person you are sizing up

1. The What:

  1. Attitude toward people in general
  2. Attitude of person toward him/herself

3. Extent of self-centeredness and use of I, me, and my rather than you
4. Attitude and treatment of superiors, peers, and subordinates
5. Positive and optimistic outlook on his/her job and life or negative and pessimistic perspective
6. Opportunity seeker and risk-taker or play it safe attitude
7. Pet peeves or turn off attitudes versus turn on and accepting of the way things are
8. Types of things that upset him/her and how the person reacts to adversity
9. Giving and receiving help, criticism, praise, frank input, and feedback
10. Things person likes and dislikes at work and off the job
11. Welcomes change or prefers status quo
12. Has strong convictions or has situational ethics
13. Attitude regarding important life events

2. Sizing up Person's Personality:

1. Primarily an introvert or extrovert
2. Pleasant and friendly or distant and aloof
3. Generally secure, confident, trusting, and open-minded versus acting defensive, anxious, suspicious, and closed-minded
4. Secure and decisive or insecure and indecisive
5. Calm and even tempered or excitable and moody
6. Level of comfort with strangers and the unknown
7. Likes as opposed to dislike of engaging in small talk
8. Primarily an evening or morning person
9. Extent he/she fits into the organization's culture
10. Importance of personal appearance to person
11. Primarily people centered or task oriented

3. Sizing Up the Person's Thought Process:

1. Determine things that are important and unimportant to person
2. Proactive and future oriented rather than past oriented and focused on day-to-day activities
3. Focuses on the big picture instead of details
4. Primarily an idea or details person
5. Mainly a theoretical or practical thinker

6. Has high work standards and strives for excellence or is content to do just enough to get by (good enough should never be good enough)
7. Fast or slow thinker
8. Emphasizes form (process) over substance (results)
9. Thought process is typically methodical and calculating rather than spontaneous and impulsive
10. Thinking is typically organized and logical versus off top of his/her head and haphazard
11. Action oriented and quick to get closure or procrastinates and slow to wrap things up
12. Prefers to work independently rather than as part of a team
13. Likes to receive conclusions and recommendations first followed by background and detailed account of something or vice versa
14. Normally is closed-minded with blind spots and prejudices rather than being open-minded and free of biases
15. Logical and objective thinker with the ability to conceptualize or lacks this ability
16. Reacts to change and uncertainty calmly and confidently as opposed to losing his/her composure and ability to think logically and objectively

4. Sizing Up Person's Knowledge and Understanding:

1. Extent of person's authority and power at work
2. Attitude toward and way uses authority
3. Intelligence and ability to comprehend what is said or written
4. Vocabulary level and words used in everyday conversation
5. Type and extent or work experience and depth of knowledge gained from this experience
6. Ability to follow and understand detailed and complex instructions

5. Sizing Up Person's Communicating Style:

1. Simple or sophisticated use of language
2. Extensive or limited vocabulary
3. Use of positive or negative words
4. Exaggerates or understates way of saying things
5. States things directly or indirectly

6. Knows and uses technical terms
7. Method of expressing him/herself: word choice, tone of voice, fluent or hesitant, confident or nervous
8. Method of expressing agreement and disagreement
9. Stresses facts versus feelings and opinions most frequently
10. How and when asks questions
11. Type and frequency of body movement
12. How person stands, sits, and walks
13. Frequency and type of eye contact—times person looks at you intently and when suddenly looks down or away from you
14. Primarily a listening or speaking person
15. Type and frequency of touching people
16. Way listens—sincerely interested or merely being polite
17. Times he/she listens most attentively

6. The How:

- To size up someone open up all your senses and focus your complete attention on the person you are sizing up
- These methods are typically used to size up a person:
  1. Be objective when sizing up a person
  2. Avoid being obvious when sizing up a person because people don't like being judged and may resent it
  3. Observe all aspects of what a person says and does
  4. Remain silent, listen carefully, and talk only to ask questions
  5. Be sure to observe representative behavior rather than limited behavior
  6. Read between the lines to detect contradictory behavior between the words being spoken and the person's facial expressions, body positions, and movement
  7. Ask person's family, friends, and coworkers questions discreetly to obtain additional information and insights

7. The When:

- To size someone fairly and accurately you need to observe his/her behavior in a variety of usual and unusual situationsYou jeopardize the validity of your sizing-up procedures if the attitudes and behavior of the person are not representative of the person's attitude and behavior The times that are recommended for sizing up a person are:

- Over a sufficient period of time rather than all at one time
- When you have time and are not rushed or under pressure
- When you are in an objective frame of mind and are not preoccupied
- When person is interacting with all kinds of people—peers, superiors, and subordinates
- Times when he/she is under pressure, in the midst of turmoil, or disagreeing with someone
- When involved in both small and large group projects
- When receiving and reacting to bad news
- When acting in both leadership and follower roles
- When person is working both alone and in groups
- When person is talking with strangers and people he/she knows well
- When the person is surprised by something and has to react quickly
- When the person has just committed a serious mistake
- When the person is receiving praise or being criticized
- During exciting special events or when engaged in routine activities
- During morning and evening hours just before and after meals
- When active and inactive, healthy or ill, and when happy and sad
- When interrupted while talking or doing something important
- When participating in structured and unstructured situations
- When engaged in routine activities compared with new ones
- When put on the spot and pressured to say something when he/she prefers to be noncommittal
- When defending an idea being strongly opposed by critics

TOPIC 11

Gaining Mutual Understanding

"When I use a word it means just what I choose
it to mean nothing more or less"
—Humpty Dumpty

A. Things to Know and Things to Do

1. Getting Understood—Essential Things to Know:

- There is no communication without understanding
- In order to succeed, a manager must understand and be understood by his superiors, subordinates, and peers
- The person speaking or writing has the primary responsibility for making him/herself clear
- Managers will enhance their chances of being understood if they get their thinking crystal clear before saying anything to anyone (it is impossible to communicate clearly to another person something that is unclear in your own mind)
- It is a mistake to assume that close and frequent contact with someone guarantees that you are going to be understood by that person—this just *ain't* so! People tend to see and hear what is important to them. People see what only they want to see and hear what they want to hear—they automatically filter out everything else
- It is both unwise and naïve to assume that you have actually said what you intended to say or that the other person understands what you've said as you intended it to be heard
- Language is constantly changing and so are the meanings of words. One of the most satisfying feelings in life is the feeling that you have been truly understood by another person

2. Impact of Personality on Understanding:

- When you are liked and respected what you say is received more favorably and understood better than when you are disliked and held in low regard
- If your image is that of a person of principle and integrity, who follows up on commitments, people will be inclined to believe you and pay close attention to what you say
- It is imperative that you show people you are sincere and genuine and that they can trust what you say
- A lively enthusiastic way of expressing yourself normally encourages a more attentive and enthusiastic reaction to your comments
- If you have an open mind and are an attentive listener other people will usually be responsive to what you have to say

3. Influence of Your Thinking and Attitude on Your Communications:

- Convey a positive attitude to the people you are communicating with and about the subject you are conversing about
- It is essential that you think carefully about what you want to say ahead of time and also about the best way to say it to promote understanding
- Be careful of making spur-of-the-moment comments off the top of your head because you may not say exactly what you intended to say and consequently will send mixed messages that confuse your listeners
- Try to speak and write clearly and simply without sounding as though you are talking down to people
- Clear thinking must precede clear expression
- People can't be expected to and won't guess at what you are trying to tell them
- View your listeners and readers as unique individuals rather than stereotyping or labeling them
- Develop feelings of commonality with your listeners and readers

4. Timing Factors to Consider:

- Bad timing interferes with getting your message understood
- Events immediately preceding or following your remarks may cause distractions and adversely affect getting your message understood

- Receivers of messages best understand what is being said to them when they feel well, feel unrushed, are free of pressure, and in a receptive mood
- Answer the question "what's in it for me" for your listeners at the beginning of your message
- Communicate with other people at the best time for them rather than the most convenient time for you

5. *Message Content:*

- Guarantee being better understood by:
  1. Telling people what you are going to tell them
  2. Telling them
  3. Telling them what you have told them
- A message is best understood when it is concrete, specific, and cites: names, places, things, and events
- Refrain from mixing important with unimportant information because it makes it harder for the listener and reader to differentiate between what is important and unimportant
- Present information in a logical order
- People tend to tune you out if you present too much information too fast
- It is important when talking with people to realize that if the information you are sharing is new or complicated that they may have a tough time understanding it
- Get directly to the point and stick to it
- Send a strong and consistent message by having your words, voice tone, volume, and body language all say the same thing
- It is advisable to consult with others to obtain their viewpoints and input in order to improve the contents of your message before sending it
- Humor that is spontaneous and related to the matter being discussed can help maintain listener's interest
- People generally react to messages with greater interest when they are important to and relate to them
- Anything you say that bolsters the listener's ego creates instant and strong interest. Conversely, when listener's self-esteem is placed in jeopardy, they lose interest and concentrate on defending themselves

6. *Wording That Enhances Your Message:*

- State the purpose of your message immediately
- Use plain and simple language that is not ambiguous
- Use picture words that create a mental image for your listeners and readers
- Be as brief as possible; eliminate all unnecessary words
- Give relevant examples, anecdotes, and explanations
- Present important, complicated, and detailed information more than once and in different ways
- Use words that are familiar to and appeal to your readers and listeners
- Avoid using slang, colloquialisms, sexist, and foreign words
- Use standard American pronunciation and avoid regional pronunciation
- Speak about one subject at a time
- Tailor your words to your listener and reader
- Emphasize important points you are making by saying such things as "this is very important so pay close attention"
- Be specific, precise, and avoid saying things that are general or vague
- Use clear and definite transitions when leaving one point to move on to the next. For example, "Now I'd like to move on to my third key point"
- Limit the amount of information you offer at one time to avoid overwhelming your listeners
- Give important information more time and emphasis
- Provide concise background information to aid understanding
- Put your most important information at the beginning and ending of your communication
- Define technical and specialized terms at the beginning of your presentation
- Invite your listeners to ask clarifying questions at any time during your presentation
- Use concrete and avoid using abstract words
- Summarize important information periodically to reinforce it and to aid retention

- Use precise wording, repetition, pause, voice variety, and obtain feedback when making an important point
- Consider using these techniques to clarify your statements:
  1. Numerous examples tailored to the interests and experience of the receivers of the message
  2. Stories, anecdotes, and case histories related to the point being made
  3. Explanations preferably with visuals to supplement your words
  4. Testimony by a person respected by the listeners
  5. Statistics that are relevant and easy to understand
- Ask yourself these questions periodically while speaking:
  1. "Am I saying things that are consistent and noncontradictory?"
  2. "Am I sending a clear or mixed message?"
  3. "Am I using precise and familiar words that are easy to understand or am I using ambiguous words that could confuse people?"
- Watch your listener's body language to determine their reactions to what you are saying
- Use lively words and avoid using tired worn-out words and sentences that have little appeal and impact
- Keep from using empty, meaningless, and superfluous words such as "kill dead" or "He has a bright future ahead of him"
- Use euphemisms and politically correct terms sparingly because they tend to water down and weaken the point you are making—you want to be sure to say things as they are, not as they aren't
- Remember to consider the context's effect on the interpretation and reaction of people receiving your message
- Speak and write with a simple and direct style that follows these rules:
  1. Prefer active to passive wording
  2. Prefer positive to negative words
  3. Prefer using only a few adverbs and adjectives instead of many
  4. Prefer personal to impersonal words
- Ask these questions to aid getting understood:
  1. What am I trying to say and why?
  2. Do I really need to say it?

      3. How can I say it most clearly?

      4. How can I make my point firmly yet tactfully?

      5. When is the best time to say it?

- Also ask yourself these questions about the receivers of especially important messages:

      1. What is their knowledge and experience with the subject?

      2. What is their attitude toward the content of the message?

      3. How much interest do they have in the topic?

      4. Do I need to provide substantial background information in order for people to be able to understand me?

- Ask these questions to verify that you have been understood:

      1. Would you repeat the essence of what I have said in your own words?

      2. "What are your reactions to what I am saying and why?"

      3. "What problems do you see with my proposal?"

      4. "Would you show me how to do what I have demonstrated for you?"

- Never just ask "do you understand?" When you ask a question, in this way people usually respond with a nod of their head or mumble "uh uh" even though they really don't have a clue about what you have said. Instead, ask questions that can't be answered with one word such as yes or no.
- You can also encourage people to answer your questions by saying something like this—"I have offered lots of new ideas and I know you must have questions—who has the first question?"

7. Selecting The Best Way to Gain and Retain People's Attention:

- Talk about people's interests, concerns, needs, and problems to get and maintain their attention
- Speak as equals and as adult to adult
- Appeal to people's insatiable curiosity or issue a low key challenge
- Stir the emotions—don't merely rely on facts to make your point and encourage follow-up action
- Tailor your communicating style or approach to the nature of the situation and your listeners

- Treat women equally and use gender-neutral words when speaking to a group of both men and women
- Be direct and realistic. Say things as they are—not as you wish they were. If you are too indirect or subtle people may miss your point
- Keep a watchful eye out and open ears for indications as to whether you are being understood or misunderstood by people
- Project your voice so it will be loud enough to be heard easily
- Articulate your speech sounds carefully and pronounce your words correctly
- Vary your pitch according to what you are saying. For example, if saying something solemn use a low pitch sound. Conversely, if talking about a joyful topic use a high pitched voice
- Speak at a lively rate (at least one hundred and twenty words a minute)
- Vary your rate of speaking to match the type or importance of the subject
- Pause periodically to:
  1. Think about what you want to say next
  2. Emphasize an important idea and
  3. Give your listeners time to digest what you have said
- Keep your throat moist and voice clear by sipping some cool (not cold) water occasionally and unobtrusively

8. *Understanding What is Said to You:*

- Managers need to seek not only to have what they have said understood by employees, but to understand what employees say to them
- Managers typically concentrate on getting understood by employees; however, it is equally important for them to understand what their employees say to them
- It is sad but true that no one person can ever totally understand what another person has said
- The same communication that is clearly understood by one person may be completely misunderstood by another person

- Meaning is totally within a person and depends upon the individual's values, perceptions, and experience. Therefore, the meaning of words is intensely personal.
- You can understand what is said to you best by attempting to view things from the speaker's perspective

9. Important Facts about Words Affecting Understanding:

- Words are subjective and inexact
- Meaning of words is in people, not in the words themselves
- Most occupations have their own technical and specialized words whose meaning is unknown and a mystery to outsiders
- Context influences meaning immensely
- Exchange of meaning is always a matter of probability rather than certainty
- Even a slight difference in words can cause anywhere from a minor to a major difference in how people interpret and react to the message
- Mark Twain once made this observation about the difference in words. "The slight difference in words can be the difference between lightning and the lightning bug"
- The meaning of words is always changing
- Words can convey one message and the person's tone of voice a different one resulting in confusion about what is really meant
- Each of us has emotional blind spots and prejudices that affect our understanding of the meaning of words
- A person seldom says exactly what he/she intends to say and this causes confusion on the part of listeners
- The difficulty of gaining understanding is compounded by a person's need to not only understand the meaning of a person's words but the feeling behind the words

10. Methods to Use to Promote Understanding:

- Keep an open mind—avoid being preoccupied and judgmental
- Stand or sit comfortably so your body is relaxed
- Concentrate on what the person is saying rather than who is saying it and how it is being said

- Be in a receptive mood and desire to understand
- Be sincerely interested in what is being said
- Focus your full attention on the person speaking by shutting out all distractions and noise
- Ignore the speaker's appearance, grooming, and mannerisms
- Avoid going on mental vacations periodically
- Hear out the person and refrain from pre-judging or jumping to conclusions
- Avoid the tendency to think about what you want to say next or how to refute what is being said by the person speaking
- Don't let inflammatory words or words you strongly dislike interfere with your listening attentively to the speaker
- Read between the lines—watch and study the speaker's body language and voice variations
- Listen for the feelings being expressed as well as to the facts and opinions
- Pick an optimal time to discuss important conceptually complex subjects
- Ask questions as needed to clarify what is being said. For example, "would you please clarify what you meant by . . . ?"
- Take brief notes on the most important things said in meetings
- Add to your vocabulary on an ongoing basis to become familiar with the meaning of more words
- Try to have a favorable opinion of the person speaking in order to be receptive to his/her comments
- Be willing to hear what people are really saying as opposed to what you want to hear or expect to hear
- Your understanding of other people will be enhanced if you understand yourself

11. *How To Show That You Understand What Was Said to You:*

- It is vital that you not only understand what people say to you but also to show them that you understand what they have said
- People need to know and have the reassurance that you understand what has been said by the way you act and the things you say

- There are several ways that you can show people that you understand what they have said. These include:
  1. Restate what the person has said in your own words. Simply re-phrase the key thoughts and feelings stated by the person speaking. For example, "As I understand it you are feeling happy today because you are going to the World Series"
  2. Mirror back what the speaker said verbatim (Although this only shows that you heard the words)
  3. Ask probing questions related to what the speaker just said to clarify or gain additional information. For example, "would you tell me more why you are excited to attend the World Series?"
  4. Making statements such as these don't show you understand but are reassuring to the person talking with you:
- "I see," "I hear you," "I understand," "I share your concern," "I agree with you"
- Make reassuring sounds without any words such as "umm hmm"
- Have facial expressions that are compatible with what the person is saying. For example, if the person is citing something that is really sad, you would have a sorry look on your face and depressed body position
- Relating an anecdote or story comparable to the person's predicament
- Summarizing the key points at the end of the discussion in this way: "let me see if I have this right—you feel unjustly criticized for failing to meet the deadline because you had no control over the power outage."
- You show that you have understood when you complete the assignment you were given by your boss.

TOPIC 12

Giving and Getting Feedback

"Men no longer test words to see what the truth is in them, the majority are only interested in knowing what their effect will be"
—Theodore Hacker

A. Things to Know

- Feedback is an essential but often overlooked component of the communicating process.
- Feedback is the only way you have of verifying that you understand something that has been said to you. Conversely, getting feedback is needed to confirm that something you have said is understood by the person listening to you.
- Nothing can be assumed when you are communicating. If the sender doesn't obtain feedback from the receiver, he/she has no clue about how well the communication was understood.
- Fortunately, in most communicating situations, the potential for receiving feedback exists.
- Feedback is most candid when the two people trust each other and have reputations as people having integrity and acting ethically.
- Effective feedback separates facts from perceptions, inferences, and opinions.
- Successful feedback requires reciprocity, leveling, and frankness.
- Face-to-face feedback is the best method because it allows information to be checked out immediately and body language can be observed.
- Changes in voice tone, loudness, pitch, and body language all provide feedback.
- Giving feedback should include the expression of feelings as well as ideas and facts.

- Speakers and writers should use as many methods for securing reliable feedback as possible.
- Giving prompt and well-timed feedback can be a plus and prevent problems whereas late and poorly timed feedback can be a minus and cause problems.
- Paraphrased feedback is far superior to feedback that is verbatim because it demonstrates that you clearly understand what was said to you rather than your ability to merely repeat words.

B. Things to Do

1. How to Get Feedback:

- Tell the employee why you need the feedback and how it will help you
- Emphasize that frank and specific feedback will be welcomed and appreciated
- Follow up on the feedback or the employees may wonder why you asked for it
- Request feedback in a polite and respectful manner rather than abruptly demanding it
- Ask questions to secure feedback instead of assuming it will be volunteered
- Pause about ten seconds after asking employees a question to enable them to think about the answer
- Restrict your questions to obtain feedback to one subject at a time
- Ask for feedback immediately after you have said something complicated or especially important
- Start with general and indirect questions and then, if needed, follow up with specific probing questions to receive feedback
- Ask relevant questions to secure feedback but avoid putting employees on the spot or embarrassing them
- Ask employees to demonstrate or explain what you have just finished demonstrating or explaining
- Explain a new procedure or exchange in routines and then ask employees what problems they can see with implementing

them. This type of feedback enables you to find out if they really understand the procedure.

- Ask employees to repeat the essence of something important you just said in their own words
- Ask this kind of question after providing lots of information at one time "I've just given you a great deal of new information that is complicated and if I were you I would have some questions, what are yours?"
- Secure group feedback to a written message by having a meeting with members of the group or you could ask them to e-mail you the questions or use the telephone hot line to get answers to their questions or concerns.
- Have the will power to be assertive when you definitely need feedback from both your superiors and employees. For example, "MrHickenlooper, could you state the reasons you are critical of my proposal?"
- Show sincere interest in receiving employee input and feedback that you consider to be necessary, important, and valuable

2. How to Give Feedback:

- View giving feedback as an opportunity not an imposition
- Take the necessary time to consider exactly what you want to say and how to say it best
- Consider the possible consequences of your answer before saying anything and how the person you are giving the feedback to will react
- Allow yourself adequate time to supply the feedback—don't rush it
- Verify that you understand the question you have been asked in order for you to give a relevant response
- Be brief—don't overwhelm the person with too much information when providing feedback
- Be as clear as possible by using plain and simple language
- Be specific instead of general, and concrete rather than abstract when giving your feedback

- Provide examples and explanations directly related to the point you are making
- Avoid judging the value of the question you have been asked when furnishing your feedback. For example, "that is an extremely important question"
- Give your feedback in a low key and tactful manner to have it received favorably
- Show that you appreciate the chance to provide feedback and the opportunity to be heard

"The Benefits of Obtaining and Responding to Employees' Ideas and Suggestions

An Idea Not The Source of an Idea is The Important Thing"
—Anonymous

A. Things to Know and Things to Do

1. Obtaining Suggestions

- Suggestion systems are a method for obtaining ideas and suggestions from employees who see things that can be improved at the workplace. They are a type of input and feedback that enable employees to proactively contribute to the organization's effectiveness.
- Suggestions could include (1) how to do things faster, better, easier, cheaper, and safer
- The most important ingredient for the success of a suggestion system is the active and enthusiastic support by managers
- There are significant benefits resulting from an effective suggestion system which include:
  1. Enables employees to feel they are a valuable and contributing member of the organization
  2. Motivates employees when they see coworkers receiving recognition and rewards
  3. Provides an effective method for upward communication
  4. Helps the workplace to be more efficient, save money, be safer, and promote morale

- There are numerous ways for managers to secure employee suggestions. These are worth considering: (1) telephone hotline, (2) suggestion boxes, (3) one-page printed suggestion form, (4) new ideas pad, (5) scheduling time for discussing suggestions, (6) e-mails to managers, (7) Delphi mailings, (8) quality circle discussions, (9) brainstorming with ideas written on a flip chart or screen and (10) group writing of ideas.
- Let's examine the basics of how each of these methods works:
  1. The telephone hotline:
     - Employees are informed that the hotline exists, its purpose, and how to use it
     - Employee calls the hotline and briefly explains his/her suggestion
     - Employee can identify him/herself or omit identifying him/herself. By identifying him/herself the employee can be contacted by management for more details, if interested
     - The response is given by the appropriate manager or chairperson of suggestion review committee
  2. Suggestion boxes
     - Several locked suggestion boxes are located strategically at heavy traffic places
     - Employees submit suggestions on the suggestions form or on a piece of paper
     - Employees have the option of stating their name or submitting the idea or suggestion anonymously
     - Boxes are opened regularly at the times the suggestion procedure requires
     - Suggestions are screened by the appropriate manager or the suggestions committee and the person who submitted the suggestion is contacted with the results of the suggestion or to get more information
  3. One-page printed form
     - Organization prints a one-page form for employees to use for making suggestions with directions on how to use it to submit suggestions

- Forms are readily available in each work unit
- Person has the option of signing his/her name or omitting it
4. New idea card:
   - Employee writes suggestion on a printed 3x5 card that allows for instant copies to be made
   - Employee sends suggestion to immediate supervisor, or person designated as organization's suggestions review committee
   - Supervisor or reviewers acknowledge receipt of suggestion within ten days along with a response to the suggestion
   - Employee contacts supervisor after ten days if he/she hasn't received a reply; the employee is informed as to the acceptance or rejection of the idea. If the idea is rejected, the employee is informed of the reason for the rejection.
5. An open door is scheduled for employees to discuss their suggestions
   - Employees explain their suggestions during the scheduled time
   - Employee is responded to in accordance with the established review procedure
6. Use of e-mail to make suggestions
   - Organization announces the e-mail address for employees to send their suggestions to
   - Employees send ideas to this address and manager in charge of the suggestions system responds to the suggestion
   - Reviewing person or group responds to employee within the time set forth by the suggestion procedure
7. The Delphi method:
   - Management selects a group of knowledgeable employees and sends them, by letter or e-mail, a clear and specific statement about a problem that it needs help solving
   - The employees, independently and without consulting anyone, submit their ideas about how to solve the problem
   - The manager requesting the help, or the management suggestion review team, selects the best answer. However, many times the answer is not acceptable the first time around.

- The manager who needs the help states the best solution proposed by the people requested to help and asks them to analyze the proposed solution and improve on it.
- The people are asked to help again by submitting their ideas building upon the proposed solution (for the second time).
- The manager reviews the suggestions from the second round. If the revised solution is acceptable the manager expresses his/her appreciation to the group and implements the proposed solution.
- The same procedure is used for each round of suggestions-Sometimes it requires several rounds of revised suggestions until a satisfactory solution is finally secured.
- Note—with the Delphi method there are no meetings and no way to identify who made which suggestions. No one can dominate the process and no personality clashes occur.

8. Quality circles discussions:
   - There are usually at least four people and a maximum of twelve people that form a quality circle. The group is typically led by the group's immediate supervisor.
   - The group usually meets for an hour or so weekly to solve work problems present in its work unit.
   - At times the quality circle meetings are attended by middle management reps who interact with members of the group.
9. Brainstorming:
10. Brainstorming is a structured meeting of a group of employees assembled to think of new ideas or ways to improve upon something already existing. The discussion occurs in an open, freed up, and nonjudgmental climate.
11. The purpose is for group members to think of as many new ideas as possible within a set time limit.
12. There are three distinct phases of brainstorming:
13. Obtaining as many ideas as possible without any judgment being made about the value or merits of the proposed idea
14. Discussion of the merits of each idea
15. Selection of the best idea
16. The adoption of rules of conduct and adhering to them is essential for any brainstorming session to succeed. The six basic

rules for brainstorming are: (1) all criticisms and judgments are ruled out (prohibited) in the first phase of the process; (2) all compliments, or criticism and reactions are prohibited in the first phase; (3) freewheeling and uninhibited expression of ideas is the goal; (4) discussion and questioning regarding any suggestion is prohibited; (5) quantity of ideas is the goal in phase 1 without any concern for quality or practicality; (6) in phase 2 building on the ideas of others is encouraged.

- The recommended method for conducting a brainstorming session is as follows:
- Secure a conference room that is private, quiet, and free of distractions
- Arrange the chairs in a semicircle facing the facilitator and flip chart
- Limit the number of participants to a minimum of five and a maximum of nine
- Three people are needed to assist with the recommended method for conducting brainstorming sessions: (1) the facilitator; (2) the flip chart recorder and (3) person to post flip chart sheets on walls.
- The facilitator reviews the ground rules with the participants.
- Participant's suggestions or ideas are recorded on the flip chart as they are offered. Each time a page on the flip chart becomes full of the participant's ideas it is removed and posted on a wall with masking tape so that the members of the group can see them easily.
- The recorder is asked to write as legibly as possible and to ask people to repeat their ideas when necessary.
- The facilitator makes sure the offering of ideas is inclusive and that no one individual dominates the proceedings or that anyone is left out of the proceedings.
- The facilitator calls for break after forty-five or sixty minutes and then resumes with phase 2 of the proceedings.
- During phase 2 the merits of the ideas are discussed and the list is narrowed down to only practical ideas.
- Phase 3 is introduced and the group proceeds to focus on the top three or four best ideas before selecting the best one.

2. Group Writing of Suggestions:

- One of the most interesting but seldom used techniques for coming up with suggestions is the group writing method.
- The group writing process basically involves these steps:
  1. The facilitator in charge of the writing session arranges the tables and chairs so that the participants in the exercise won't be able to hear comments being made by participants at the nearby tables.
  2. The facilitator divides the large group of participants into subgroups of four to six employees and assigns them to a table and appoints a group leader for each subgroup.
  3. The facilitator then gives all participants a writing tablet and instructs them to write their suggestions independently without saying anything to anyone else at the table. The facilitator also instructs the participants to refrain from being concerned about writing style, spelling, and punctuation, and instead to concentrate on wording the suggestion clearly.
  4. The facilitator next asks the participants to write their names and the subject of their suggestion on a tablet.
  5. The facilitator then requests that the sheets not be torn off the tablet so that all of the comments remain together. The facilitator next instructs the participants to write about their suggestion for about thirty minutes.
  6. The participants then concentrate on writing their ideas for the designated period of time.
  7. After the first writing phase is completed the participants are requested to place all their tablets on the center of their table and next trade tablets with the participants at another table.
  8. The participants at the various tables then trade tablets and are requested to write their comments about the suggestions made by people at other tables.
  9. The process of reading the suggestions by the participants at the various tables continues until each member of all the groups has read the suggestions and commented on them.
  10. The task of analyzing and reporting on the total suggestions is assigned to a monitoring team which reports its findings to the

whole group at a later date or the facilitator may decide to have the subgroups evaluate the suggestions immediately followed by the groups discussing the ideas and then conclude the proceedings by making some final recommendations.

3. Manager's Responses to Suggestions

- A manager's responses to suggestions from employees can encourage or discourage their interest in sharing their ideas with managers. It may be helpful to examine the types of responses that encourage or discourage the offering of suggestions by employees.

  1. These comments motivate employees to offer suggestions:
- "Thank youYour suggestion is an excellent one."
- "Let's see how we can make your suggestion work."
- "Great idea! Let's give it a try."
- "It isn't in the budget, but I think I can switch some money around and use your idea."
- "Interesting—let's discuss the key points of your idea."
- "We can always bend policy a little for an idea such as this."
- "It may be tough to implement your idea but it's worth a try."

  2. These kinds of responses are idea killers:
- "We tried that before and it didn't work."
- "We don't have time for something like that now."
- "It's not in the budget so we can't do anything new."
- "Why change? We are doing okay now."
- "You may be right but we've always done it this way."
- "Your idea could set a dangerous precedent."
- "We have all we can do now."
- "It's against policy."

  3. Rejecting suggestions diplomatically:
- When managers have to turn down employee's suggestions it is advisable for them to do the following:
- Show they understand the suggestion and that they have given it careful thought
- Respond within a reasonable period of time

- Explain the reasons you need to reject the suggestion
- Express your appreciation for the employee's desire to be helpful
- Invite the employee to continue to make suggestions
- Drop by the employee's work area a couple of days after you have rejected his/her suggestion to engage in some friendly small talk

TOPIC 14

Dealing Compassionately With Employee's Feelings

"Holding it in creates horrid poisons which wear us out before our time"

—Robertson Davies

A. Things to Know

- Employee's attitude and feelings directly affect his/her job performance.
- As much as managers might like to leave employee's personal feelings out of their relationship and business discussions, this is not a realistic option.
- When discussing something managers need to accept the fact that no meeting or discussion can be effective without addressing the emotional needs of both the manager and his/her employees.
- Experiencing and expressing emotions to another person is not only desirable but essential for the well-being of all the people involved.
- Many managers pride themselves on being objective and down playing feelings while carrying out their daily duties. However, this attitude can cause serious problems with employees because effective communication requires sharing not only facts but feelings.
- We are all emotional beings and our feelings affect all of our communications. We cannot turn our feelings off irrespective of how much we might want to.

- For another person to respond effectively to another person's feelings he/she must first know what the feelings are.
- It is appropriate for people to show their feelings when speaking and listening. However, at work, people need to strive to control their emotions. Control is most difficult when the manager and his/her employees disagree strongly on a matter.
- If individuals who disagree on important issues honestly express their feelings and sincerely listen to each other's feelings on the matter, they will be able to understand each other's viewpoints better.
- A person needs to avoid confusing what he/she feels with the actual situation.
- An employee's willingness to share his/her feelings with a manager is an indication that he/she enjoys a positive and trusting relationship with that manager.
- People have two ways to communicate their feelings: (1) verbally and (2) nonverbally by their bodily actions.
- People need to send the same message by their words and body language because if they send mixed messages they will confuse people listening to them.
- When a person's words and body language are sending different messages, the person's body language is probably sending the truest message (please note a more detailed account of nonverbal is presented elsewhere in this book).
- To understand and accept the feelings of people requires that managers have the desire and ability to be empathetic.
- An empathetic person has the ability to perceive and feel the emotions of the other person essentially in the same way as the other person is experiencing them.
- Each business discussion has three types of interactions: (1) ideas; (2) facts; and (3) feelings.
- Since people react to emotions being expressed more than to facts, managers must be careful to give feelings their due attention and to never underestimate the power of their influence.
- Strong feelings can create harm if held in. Therefore, it is best to encourage the person to express his/her feelings immediately.

B. Things to Do

- Managers need to control their feelings when interacting with employees in pressure-packed situations.
- By listening intently and nonjudgmentally, managers empower their employees to express their most heartfelt feelings.
- Managers can help their employees to deal more effectively with their on-the-job problems by giving them a chance to express how they feel about various work-related problems.
- Managers encourage employees to state their feelings when they listen silently, patiently, and without interrupting them.
- Managers need to permit employees to air their gripes and negative feelings openly rather than trying to suppress them.
- Managers need to respond to the feelings aspect of a discussion rather than focusing only on the intellectual or factual content of a discussion.
- It is risky for managers to merely assume to know their employee's thoughts and feelings. Managers need to check out their perceptions to guarantee that they really understand their employee's feelings.
- Managers need to state what they believe are the feelings expressed by their employees and wait for the employees to confirm that the manager's perception was correct or needs to be clarified.
- When a manager is listening to a highly emotional employee he/she needs to control his/her own emotions and to show compassion for the person. Usually the best thing a manager can do is to remain silent, be interested, and act like a sponge so the employee can let off steam. Managers may want to be fully involved but they must realize if they get too involved they may lose their objectivity and be in danger of taking over the problem and making it their own.
- If the employee's emotional outbursts become too frequent, managers need to consider advising the employee to secure the services of a professional, such as a therapist.
- A manager's judgmental statements inhibit the employee's desire and ability to share his/her feelings. Therefore, it is

wise to respond by using neutral words and mirroring the employee's feelings and comments or paraphrase what the employee has just finished saying.

- When a manager understands how things appear to the employee, he/she feels more willing to modify his/her position to one more closely aligned with that of the employee.

- Managers need to develop the sensitivity to observe and detect subtle changes in an employee's behavior while speaking, listening, and paying close attention to the employees word choices, loudness or pitch of voice, facial expressions, and body positioning and movement.

- In situations where the employee is encountering difficulty in putting his/her feelings into words, a manager can help by saying things like this:
  1. "Let me see if this is what you are trying to say?"
  2. "Is this what you are getting at?"
  3. "I am eager to hear what you have to say and I am here for you, so relax, take your time, and say what you want to say"
  4. "Feel free to say what you want to say—I will hold everything you tell me in the strictest of confidence."

- Avoid interrupting the person or substituting your words for the employees as this can be insulting.

- Use words that have special appeal to the employee and do not push his/her hot buttons. Conversely, if you have any doubts about how the employee will react to certain words, don't use them. For example, avoid using the word liberal if the employee is an ardent conservative politically or don't use profanity when talking to a highly religious person.

- Managers can react to an employee's feelings in a supportive way by saying such things as:
  1. "Yes, I agree with you."
  2. "I can certainly see why you feel as you do."
  3. "If I were in your shoes I would probably feel the same way you do."
  4. "I think you did exactly the right thing."

Note: Managers make a dangerous and ill-advised statement when they say, "I know exactly how you feel" or "everything will be okay, I just know that it will" or "It is God's will so you don't need to worry about anything."

- In addition to knowing what to say to a troubled employee, it is equally important to know what not to say
- It is wise to avoid saying the following:
  1. "Hold on! I want you to calm down and control yourself."
  2. "I'm not going to sit here and listen to you carry on like this."
  3. "I know exactly how you feel."
  4. "You are talking nonsense and I want you to stop it right now."
  5. "I'm not going to listen to this—come back later when you've calmed down."
  6. "I don't know where you got such a crazy idea—now get control of yourself and talk sense."
  7. "There is no use for you to feel so upset—you're making a mountain out of a mole hill."

1. Things to Avoid Doing

1. Interrupting the employee with your own comments—the manager's thoughts and feelings are of little or no importance at this time
2. Showing impatience, irritation, or anger
3. Looking amused or making light of the situation
4. Looking bored, preoccupied, or inattentive
5. Trying to change the subject
6. Responding emotionally
7. Acting disapprovingly or shocked
8. Glancing at your watch frequently and acting rushed
   - Sometimes you may notice an employee acting emotional while working and yet he/she has not asked for help. In these situations you can go to the person and say: "I sense you are feeling upset this morning, would you like to talk about it? I'm available to listen if you want to talk about it."
   - One of the fundamental needs of all human beings is to be noticed, listened to, and understood. By ignoring a person's feelings you are ignoring the essence of the person.

TOPIC 15

Strategies of Being Noncommittal

"In Silence Also There's a Worth That Brings no Risks"
—Simonides of Ceos

A. Things to Know

- Knowing how to answer or how to avoid answering questions graciously is crucial for managers.
- Being noncommittal means you avoid stating your views, taking a position, or giving a definite answer to a question you have been asked.
- A touchy or sensitive issue is one that is emotion charged and one that requires great care and tact when being discussed.
- Managers do not need to feel obligated to respond to everything said to them or asked of them. The situation and possible consequences of an answer to questions determines whether a manager decides to answer a question or remains noncommittal.
- If you have nothing helpful to say, it is best to say nothing.
- Generally it is a good idea to respond to what a person asks you, especially if the questioner is a member of the news media.
- Responding to a question is both the tactful and the appropriate thing to do. However, there are times that it is wise to avoid making a direct response to a question— especially if it would put you on the spot or create problems.
- Common sense, sound judgment, the type of situation and your relationship with the person asking the question should guide your decision as to whether it is best to reply or remain silent.
- A manager's noncommittal or evasive response to a question, if offered tactfully and politely, usually won't create serious problems.

- It is important when being noncommittal to ask yourself "do I have a legitimate reason for refusing to answer this question?" If not, answer the question.
- Refuse to answer speculative questions by saying "it would be improper and irresponsible for me to answer a hypothetical question."
- Managers have often regretted what they have said but rarely their silence.
- When declining to answer a question say: "it would be improper for me to answer the question" rather than saying "the question is improper so I can't answer it" (this is only a slight difference in wording but a big difference in meaning and impact).
- There are certain kinds of topics that managers prefer to be noncommittal about. These include:
  1. Information of a personal nature
  2. Classified information
  3. Confidential information
  4. Proprietary information such as plans, products, services lay-offs, and expansion
  5. Beware of questions about major changes in the organization's: mission, top level management, policies, and operating procedures.
- There are times when it is wise to be noncommittal. These are the times:
  1. You don't know the answer.
  2. You prefer to delay your answer.
  3. You know the answer but you are not free to divulge it.
  4. You prefer a more appropriate person to answer it.
  5. You want the person to answer his/her own question.
  6. You can only give a partial answer at the time.

B. Things to Do

- Your goal when being noncommittal is to minimize the risk of saying the wrong thing. When giving high-risk answers your goal is to give answers that say little or nothing without being obvious and your questioners failing to detect that you really are not saying anything about the question.

- Do your best not to act secretive or do anything that suggests you are trying to cover up a serious problem or something dangerous.
- These five guidelines for answering questions may be helpful:
  1. Ask yourself if it is ethical and proper to share the requested information at this time.
  2. Ask yourself if giving the answers is consistent with the organization's: communications philosophy, policies, and procedures—if it is yes, provide the information, if not don't give it.
  3. Ask yourself whether the consequences of sharing the information will be positive or negative.
  4. Ask yourself if the time is right for revealing the information.
  5. Ask yourself "Do I have complete, correct and current information on the subject topic of the question?"
- Using qualifying words provides you with an out if your answers result in a problem. Frequently used qualifying words are generally, usually, sometimes, frequently, rarely, seldom, normally, and maybe. Qualifying phrases include: "it depends," "all things being equal," "I really don't know but my guess is," "maybe yes and maybe no—it all depends."
- There are times when it is both appropriate and inappropriate to use qualifying words and phrases in any event. Qualifiers should be used judiciously or your credibility may suffer.
- Take both sides of an issue when both sides of the issue have merit. The advantages and disadvantages of each side should be presented fairly and objectively.
- Look and sound sincere and convincing when answering all questions.
- It is a good idea to give as much information as you can when answering questions (questioners can appreciate this).
- When you are pinned down and have to answer a question that you don't want to answer, play the politician's game—sound authoritative, use a convincing tone of voice, and impressive sounding words. Also present lots of irrelevant background and facts. Speak in generalities and change the subject without being obvious.

- There are an infinite number of honorable, tactful, and noncommittal statements that you can make. In all instances it is advisable to briefly pause to consider the best thing to say under the current circumstances.
- Make it a habit to be as open, candid, and sincere as possible when communicating with your coworkers.
- Play it safe when communicating about touchy and controversial subjects. Read a carefully prepared written statement word for word to guarantee that you actually say what you intend to say. Be sure not to deviate from your prepared text (make several copies of your written statement for the record).

Tips for Using Noncommittal Methods:

1. How to delay giving an answer;
   - Follow this admonition by Cervantes "Think before thou speakest."
   - You can't recall words once uttered but you can always contact the person who asked a question later.
   - Delay is preferable to saying something wrong. It is advisable to delay answering until you receive authorization to speak about something, get more information or need time to think.
   - You are entitled to be noncommittal until you get all the facts and have time to consider them.
   - Delay answering a question you consider presumptuous rather than refusing to answer it outright. Explain why you can't answer the question at the time but pledge to provide the answer as soon as appropriate (you are ethically obligated to honor this pledge within a reasonable time).
   - These kinds of delayed responses are usually effective:
     1. "It would not be right for me to comment on that right now, let me get back to this later."
     2. "What you have asked me is too important for me to respond to off the top of my head, I'll need time to think about it."
2. How to respond when you know the answer to a question, but don't want to answer it. For example:
   1. You can change the subject smoothly by stating "your question reminds me of a similar situation . . ."

    2. "I'm sorry I am not in a position to say anything about that today."

    3. "I can't give you a precise answer so I'd rather not say anything about it."

3. How to respond when you want the questioner to answer his/her own question

    1. "Please tell me more about that."

    2. "That's a provocative question. Why are you asking it?"

4. What to say when you don't know enough to answer:

    1. It is wise to neither guess nor bluff an answer.

    2. "I'm not sure about that so I think it is best that I say nothing about it."

    3. "I don't know the facts about that so I prefer not to guess at an answer—sorry."

    4. "hmm, that's the sixty-four thousand question isn't it?"

5. How to decline answering a question because it would be more appropriate for someone else to answer it:

- Sometimes you will be asked a question that another person knows more about than you do or who should answer it because of organizational protocol. In such instances these answers would be appropriate:

    1. I think you would be better off asking Mr. Smarts the answer to that question since he is an authority on the subject.

    2. "I'm sorry your question is out of my field. I suggest you contact Ms. Sharp to get a more informed answer."

    3. "I am sorry but I'm not the right person to answer that question. Let me give you the names of several people who are qualified to help you."

6. Providing only partial answers:

- Sometimes it is advisable to furnish only a partial answer either deliberately or because complete information is unavailable.

- Offer the limited information you have but emphasize that it is incomplete information and may contain significant omissions.

- "I'll be happy to share the limited information I have, but I don't have all the information myself. If more information becomes available I'll be happy to share it with you."

7. Answering questions without really saying anything:
   - Sometimes a manager may not want to answer a question but circumstances demand that he/she respond to a question.
   - Your goal in these situations is to appear to cooperate but actually to say nothing specific or important.
   - Provide such a long, involved, and detailed answer that the person asking the question gets lost halfway through your answer (good models for you to emulate are most experienced politicians).
   - Speak so generally and state things so indirectly that what you say is essentially meaningless.
   - "My answer to that is maybe yes or maybe no—it depends on the situation."
   - "My guess is that what you have said is generally true, but there are many exceptions to consider."
8. Making yourself deliberately unavailable:
   - When you predict that a person will be looking for you to answer several tough questions and your answers could result in some serious problems for you regardless of your answers, it is sometimes wise to make yourself physically unavailable to contact until things cool down or you have an opportunity to get advice and prepare your answers so you become less vulnerable.

TOPIC 16

Protecting Confidential Information

"A secret's safe twixt you, me and the gatepost"
—Robert Browning

A. Things to Know

1. All employees of an organization, especially managers, need to have a clear understanding of the nature of confidential information and the ways to treat and protect it. As Cervantes wisely said, "mums the word."
   - The importance of protecting confidential information cannot be overemphasized.
   - Confidential information should have restricted use and to be limited only to authorized staff.
   - Confidential material should only be viewed and discussed by those whose official functions or legal status requires them to be informed about such information.
   - Protecting confidential information should be a high priority for all managers and employees.
   - Ethical people with integrity, respect, and honor the need for keeping confidential material confidential.
   - Do not assume that all people will always keep information confidential. Too many people want to be "in the know" and like to share the "inside scoop" to make themselves feel important.
   - Disciplinary action must be prompt and severe when any member of an organization discloses confidential information.
2. Serious consequences can result if you reveal confidential information to the wrong people, such as:
   - People will no longer trust you with confidential information (or possibly anything else)

- People may question your overall trustworthiness (integrity or credibility)
- You and other people involved may feel embarrassed and humiliated by the disclosure
- You could be severely disciplined or even fired
- You could harm your reputation and jeopardize your career and the careers of other parties involved in the leak
- The organization's operational effectiveness could suffer
- There could be grave economic consequences if the information leak aids competitors

B. Things to do:

1. Be constantly vigilant and follow recommended safeguarding procedures of the organization which should include:
   - Educate employees on how to handle and guard confidential information
   - Explain why the information is confidential and the serious problems that could result from its disclosure to unauthorized people
   - Define the nature of confidential information to all employees and list the confidential material they are or will be dealing with
   - Point out the disciplinary action that will occur for violating the organization's security procedures
   - When people appear to be "pumping" you for information that they are not authorized to have, be aware of your facial expressions, body language, voice tone, and even your silence as you work to remain noncommittal
   - Assure those who seek the information prematurely that you will share the information as soon as possible
   - Allow only authorized employees access to sensitive or confidential material. Try to limit access to as few people as possible to minimize the risks of unintentional disclosure
   - Keep confidential information in a secure and restricted area to limit or prevent access
   - Keep confidential papers in folders and out of sight when you are not working with them. Be sure to lock up all confidential information, especially on evenings and weekends

- Refrain from making or retaining unnecessary or numerous copies of confidential materials
- Avoid leaving originals or copies of confidential material at the copy center
- Destroy notes, rough drafts, or poor copies by shredding them right away
- Do not toss confidential papers into waste paper containers
- Prohibit the photocopying of confidential material

2. Here are some tips for protecting confidential information shared during meetings:
   - Prior to the meeting you need to know who will attend and that all those present have the proper clearance to view and discuss the confidential information you will present
   - Tell the meeting participants at the start of the meeting that the information to be discussed is confidential and should not be discussed elsewhere
   - Prohibit note taking or recording any part of the meeting proceedings

3. Other safeguards commonly practiced to keep information confidential include:
   - Be certain that phone calls on sensitive matters can't be overheard. Make sure that neither party has his or her speaker phone turned on
   - You and your administrative assistant should review your office's security procedures together to be sure you are "on the same page"
   - Check and double check that the organization has the latest security information and operating procedures in place to safeguard confidential information
   - Watch what you say in public, especially social events where alcoholic beverages are served and your guard is down
   - Avoid discussing confidential matters with strangers or even coworkers in public places (remember the slogan, "loose lips sink ships")
   - Refrain from reading confidential information in public places where people may be sitting close to you, such as buses, planes, subways, or trains

- Think before you speak and choose your words wisely to avoid a "slip of the tongue" when talking about matters closely related to confidential information

2. Protecting Computerized Confidential Information

A. Things to Know:

1. Top management and governing boards, both in the private and public sectors, need to make the protection of confidential information a top priority
   - Cyber-security is the job of everyone in an organization. All employees need to learn the signs that indicate hacking and to realize the dangers of computer system breaches
   - Human resource departments face new challenges. They need to understand the risks of potential data breaches, have an action plan ready to prevent the breaches, and be prepared for responding effectively when a breach occurs
   - Safety measures are crucial for all sizes and types of organizations
   - All protection systems are vulnerable and organizations must work continuously to minimize the vulnerability
   - Computer system breaches are becoming more frequent and more intrusive causing disruptions that cost time and money to correct
   - Prevention of hacking is a major challenge to both government and private industry because new spyware like "zero day exploits" is difficult to guard against
   - The staff responsible for computer security should report directly to top management
   - Organizations need to install multiple safeguards against cyber-attacks because hackers have multiple ways to penetrate networks. Effective defenses against past hackers does not mean you are safe from future attacks as hackers are constantly changing their methods of attack
   - The world's most competent computer specialists are unable to identify and employ effective methods to protect confidential information 100% against all hacking

- To beat the hackers, organizations need to think as hackers do and take all necessary actions to try to outmaneuver the hackers
- Employees using computers regularly that contain confidential information need to receive comprehensive and ongoing training on how best to safeguard confidential material

2. There are sources available to assist organizations in the protecting of confidential electronic information. These include:
   - Computer consultants
   - University professors specializing in computer technology
   - Experienced computer sales representatives
   - Computer websites
   - The staff of professional associations or other organizations such as The Center of Strategies and International Studies, 1616 Rhode Island Ave., NW, Washington, DC (telephone 202-887-0200)
   - Government and other organizations trying to combat cyber-attacks are hampered by privacy issues and until the American people reach consensus on what they will permit the government to do, the problem will continue

3. Typically the computer specialist is responsible for evaluating and recommending ways to improve the organization's risk management and control system. Other duties include:
   - Conduct training session for computer users
   - Checking out and clearing new employees
   - Setting up and overseeing the computer network
   - Developing all computer security protocol
   - Determining who has access to different kinds of confidential information
   - Briefing computer users on new developments for combating cyber-attacks and any new problems being encountered

4. Common practices of small and mid-sized organizations:
   - Many organizations outsource most of their internal computer security tasks because the outside firms have more technological expertise than what is available in-house
   - Many small businesses do not have a computer network. Often they will link two or more computers and use the security provided by Microsoft or other programs or online vendors

- Most small or mid-sized businesses do not store credit card numbers and are not usually targeted by hackers
- Mid-sized or even larger businesses will take advantage of their Network provider's security programs and feel sufficiently secure
- Mega chain stores such as Home Depot, Lowes, Walmart, Target, and Kohl's typically have both in-house and out-sourced security systems

B. *Things to Do*

1. It is critical to protect computer systems in your organization from security breaches. Some suggestions to accomplish this include:
   - Secure the support of top management for the security system
   - Develop a protection system tailored for your organization
   - Adopt clear and specific protective policies and procedures with the advice of a competent computer specialist
   - Provide an adequate budget for the purchase, maintenance, and security of computers
   - Offer training for those using computers with an emphasis on how best to protect confidential information
   - Identify the information that is regarded as confidential
   - Organizations need to identify their areas of vulnerability with input from both in-house and outside computer experts
   - Build into the contract with outside computer consultants specific provisions for ongoing service and the scheduling of regular update sessions and a preview of the information that will be shared at those sessions
   - Install multiple safeguards knowing that hackers have numerous ways and means to penetrate networks
   - Explain the importance of keeping confidential information strictly confidential and offer guidelines on how to protect that information
   - Promote security by using separate rooms for securing computers with limited access and locked doors
   - Define the procedure for destroying (shredding) confidential hard copy information
   - Create back-up systems

- Select and protect passwords with due diligence
- Establish a procedure for removing computer hardware from a secure room and dealing with the software (programs) that contains the information
- Identify the worst-case scenario re: theft of confidential information that would aid competitors. Develop an effective response and test the effectiveness of that plan
- Create a list that spells out all actions considered to be violations of the organization's security procedures
- Be sure all newly hired employees, computer repair and maintenance personnel, and custodians with access to computers have had a background check or are bonded
- Hold regular meetings between the in-house computer service manager and top management to keep "the boss" informed of important computer-related matters and to address any concerns management may have about computer security

2. Here are several computer security tips that small businesses should find helpful:
   - Managers are well advised to ask themselves "who are my adversaries?" This question can help managers spot their organization's vulnerabilities and help them understand which measures to take to protect company software and hardware
   - Make sure your code is clean. Security software companies can help you identify and fix any problems with your applications source code
   - Outsource your security operation. There are many service companies that have the size and "know-how" to protect the sensitive data of small organizations. Make sure the company you outsource has the capabilities you require. However, it is imperative that you understand that employing an outside security firm does not relieve you of all your security responsibilities.
   - Buy Cyber insurance in addition to outsourcing your security needs and be sure the computer service providers can meet the

requirements of the insurance policy. One of your jobs will be to prevent internal negligence as it pertains to computers and confidential information.

Please note: much of the information presented on confidential information was obtained from computer specialists writing for the Wall Street Journal.

TOPIC 17

Creating a Healthy Communications Climate

"We are interested in others when they are interested in us"
—Publilius Syrus

A. Things to Know

- One of the toughest challenges facing managers today is to develop and maintain a work climate that will enhance communicating between managers and employees.
- Effective communication is encouraged when a favorable climate exists. Although it is the responsibility of all employees to assist in creating a wholesome climate, it is managers who must set the tone for effective communication throughout the organization.
- A significant gap exists between how most managers communicate and how most employees want to be communicated with.

1. Recommended communications attitudes for managers:
   - View employees as good, decent, and valuable people who have dignity and should be treated with respect.
   - Recognize and respect the differences among employees and that the dignity of people is in their uniqueness.
   - Project an attitude of caring about the employees, themselves, as well as an interest in their work.
   - Perceive employees as coworkers and emphasize that we attitude and team approach when working together.
   - Have a genuine concern for the needs and problems of employees.
   - Believe that employees can be trusted and have confidence in their ability to do what is right.
   - Try to know employees as people and use their names when talking with them—be sure to pronounce their names correctly.

- Be willing to be readily available to employees when they need to talk with you.
- Have a realistic outlook toward employees' performance and have them strive for excellence, not perfection.
- Seek to understand employees as well as to get understood by them.
- Have an open mind and a nonjudgmental mind-set when communicating with employees.
- Be willing to hear and act on employee's ideas and suggestions or explain your reasons for not being able to do so.
- Listen to employees without jumping to conclusions, prejudging or tuning them out.
- Allow employees to share bad news with you without "shooting the messenger."
- Share bad as well as good news candidly with employees.
- Be concerned with what is right rather than who is right when disagreeing with employees and vice versa.
- Desire to be ethical at all times and about all things with all employees.
- Have sufficient confidence to admit when you don't know something or when you make mistakes.
- Strive to share information promptly, accurately, and fully with employees.
- Talk with—not to or at—employees.
- Have a goal of treating employees fairly rather than equally because treating unequal people equally is both unfair and ineffective.
- Treat your employees as they want to be treated not as you want to be treated because your needs and theirs are different.
- Try to think positively and have an optimistic outlook when interacting with employees (but also be realistic).
- Intend to keep your promises and commitments to employees (if you can't, explain why you can't honor them and express regret).
- Bear in mind the importance of "the little things" to employees.
- Focus on what you and your coworkers can agree on rather than what you disagree about and do your best to reconcile your

differences (accept the fact that some disagreement and friction are a normal part of life at the workplace).

- Strive to be consistent and predictable so employees will know what to expect and aren't surprised by your actions.
- Desire to communicate in a way that employees feel informed, especially in times of uncertainty and change.
- Do your best to treat employees as individuals rather than labeling or stereotyping them.
- Desire to receive feedback regularly so you can check on the accuracy of your perceptions of people, things, and events.
- Accept the fact that it is better to overcommunicate than communicate too little with your coworkers so long as it isn't to excess.
- Have the courage to level with employees when necessary but have the sensitivity to do so without leveling the person in the process.
- Be willing to be flexible with your style of communicating so you can improve your chances of getting on your employees wavelength.
- Try to make each employee feel needed by and important to you and the organization.

B. Things to Do

1. Recommended communications behavior by managers:
   - Be friendly and approachable to employees and be perceived as such by the employee.
   - Show employees that they are important and feed their egos by showing you know the "little things" about them, show interest in their families and other things the employees are especially interested in.
   - Keep visible and hold "how is it going chats" (your engaging in small talk with employees is important to them).
   - Greet employees with a big smile and by name whenever you see them (know their first and last names and even their nicknames (remember one's name is like gold onto one's ears).

- Deal with employees as a fellow adult and from an "I'm okay and you are okay position."
- Act relaxed, be tactful and polite when conversing with your employees—don't rush your interactions with them.
- Make time available to go out of your way to notice people and to maintain contact with them.
- Help your employees to feel relaxed and safe around you. Talk about things they are interested in, be a good listener, and kid around some.
- Involve your employees in things such as planning, decision-making, and how to implement changes.
- Establish a feeling of commonality, togetherness, and teamwork.
- Demonstrate that people work with you and not for you—avoid an air of superiority.
- Help employees to feel free to speak up and express themselves and then listen carefully to what they are saying.
- Keep employees informed; let them know what you expect, where they stand and how they are doing; help them to feel secure.
- Assign new employees a buddy to show them the ropes and to introduce them to coworkers and the organization's culture.
- Allow employees to share gut level feelings and to ventilate about their problems in an acceptable manner (we all have bad days).
- Be cooperative and help employees when they need help.
- Control malicious rumors promptly and effectively, especially those that are harmful to employees.
- Minimize differences in status, positions, and seniority of employees when interacting with them.
- Refrain from being invasive and protect employee's rights of privacy. Protect anything employees tell you that is confidential.
- Communicate in a manner that makes employees feel listened to, understood, and responded to.
- Assist new employees to be assimilated into the organization's culture and to feel "at home," needed, and important.

- Set ambitious but attainable goals and standards for employees.
- Help employees to be successful and to realize their potential.
- Be helpful to employees but not overly so—employees need and like the freedom to do their jobs.
- Keep employees informed of changes affecting their jobs and the reasons for changes (avoid, if possible, changes that are too fast or massive).
- Let employees know when you are extremely busy, rushed, and prefer not to be disturbed—except for emergencies.
- View your management position as one of service to rather than power over people (avoid issuing commands and ordering people around).
- Speak to employees with a pleasant conversational voice tone.
- Explain to employees why their job is important and how they fit into the overall operation of the organization so they will feel important and proud of their job.
- Make sure that clear channels of communication exist and are effective (allow out of channel communicating when it makes sense to do so).
- Provide employees opportunities for both input and feedback on matters affecting their jobs.
- Seek and be responsive to new ideas and suggestions.
- Ensure that no employee is favored or discriminated against.
- Create a work environment that is relaxed but business like (avoid doing things that make employees feel tense and uptight).
- Help employees to feel like members of a team and that they are supported and backed by management.
- Deal with serious conflicts promptly and discuss them candidly.
- Help employees to feel needed and appreciated by management.
- Allow employees to use their own methods of doing their job so long as they achieve the desired results and as long as the methods are safe, sanitary, and don't cause problems for coworkers or management.
- Explain the purposes and procedures of the performance evaluation system so that employees understand and accept them.

- Encourage employees to feel free to discuss their problems, admit their mistakes, and to ask for assistance whenever they need it.
- Discuss employees job responsibilities, goals, priorities, and results jointly annually and as needed.
- Enforce sexual harassment and sexist language policies fairly and impartially.
- Make a genuine effort to tailor communications to the various diverse groups of employees.
- Give employee communication a top priority and be certain that communication is ongoing rather than sporadic, specific instead of general, concrete rather than abstract, and candid instead of politically correct.

TOPIC 18

Communicating Attitudes and Techniques that Motivate Employees

"A word fitly spoken is like applies of gold in a setting of silver"
—Solomon

A. Things to Know

1. Managers Attitudes:

- Willing to be available to employees
- Goal is to motivate not manipulate employees
- View management as service to not power over employees
- Positive and optimistic feelings toward work, employees, and the organization
- Opportunity seeker rather than problem finder
- Open-minded and receptive to changes
- Accepting and nonjudgmental feelings about employees
- Helpful and supportive
- Predictable and avoids big surprises
- Patient and self-controlled
- Notices "the little things" and considers them important
- Talks as an equal to employees
- Free of biases toward minority individuals and groups
- Likes coworkers and views him/herself as a member of the team
- Other person-centered rather than self-centered
- Is trustworthy and trusts employees
- Interacts with coworkers cooperatively and believes that employee input and feedback are important

- Expects excellent performance by employees instead of demanding perfection
- Expects and tolerates mistakes by self and by employees

B. Things to Do

2. *Techniques:*

- Keep employees informed
- Provide advance notice
- Supply ongoing rather than sporadic communications
- Level with and give constructive criticism
- Let employees know how they are doing and where they stand
- Treat employees with dignity and as unique individuals
- Treat others as they want to be treated—not as you want to be treated
- Explain the freedom and authority employees have to do their job
- Encourage employees sharing ideas and making suggestions
- Manage by wandering around and by having an open-door policy
- Announce the employee of the month and take the person to lunch
- Offer "atta boys/girls" at meetings to acknowledge employee accomplishments
- Give a pep talk and express appreciation at annual meeting
- Maintain up-to-date job descriptions with input from employees
- Jointly set annual performance goals
- Conduct fair performance evaluations
- Discuss ways employee's jobs can be enriched
- Delegate responsibilities and assign multitasks to help employees develop skills to help them reach their potential
- Praise employees promptly when recognition is due
- Give employees credit for noteworthy achievements
- Respect employees' privacy rights

- Seek to understand as well as to get understood by employees
- Speak plain and familiar language; be comfortable to be around
- Listen to employees' verbal and body language
- Engage in small talk and discuss matters of common interest with employee
- Acknowledge communications you receive from employees promptly, especially e-mails and phone calls
- Request things from employees rather than ordering or commanding them to do things
- Protect confidences and confidential information diligently
- Be reliable by making sure your words and actions match
- Mix with employees and their families at the organization's social events

Breaking Down Manager-Employee Barriers with Small Talk

"Talk in terms of your employees' interests"
—Dale Carnegie

A. Things to Know

1. Informal conversations or "small talk" with colleagues or acquaintances from other organizations can be a frequent occurrence and whether by intent or coincidental, a fair amount of business can be conducted during these conversations.

2. Most of these "watercooler" conversations are spontaneous and happen when one or more individuals see the opportunity to grab another person's attention for a few moments to actually discuss business outside of one's office.

3. Because of location and time restraints, small talk is usually brief but focused and sometimes results in a mutual agreement to meet and discuss the subject further in a more formal setting and possibly with others in attendance.

4. The locations for these "small talk" conversations are many and varied. Some examples include:

   a. Walking to and from the parking lot (or in the parking lot itself)
   b. In a break room or in the designated smoking area
   c. At the watercooler or in the copy room
   d. In the restroom
   e. In the cafeteria line or sitting together during lunch
   f. Passing in the hallway
   g. At social events outside work or at work-related social events such as picnics, family field days, or holiday parties

h. While traveling together (depending on the time available, this opportunity to converse may be substantial and can be more in depth)

i. In the organization's fitness center (usually right before or right after work day)

B. Things to Do

1. Start the conversation with light topics even if you have a purpose or subject matter you wish to chat about

2. Keep in mind this may not be the right time and place for a more substantive conversation of a serious nature

3. Talk in terms of the other person's interests

4. Start with common subjects such as sports, news events, the weather, family news, hobbies you may have in common, a complimentary comment you make about the person's new car, clothing, haircut, etc.

5. Be brief with opening comments or statements and then listen to the response to see if your idea of "small talk" is being well received

6. Sometimes begin with a question to open the conversation. "What's new?" "How's it going?" or "How is the family?"

7. Avoid discussing your problems and steer the other person away from serious complaining about the organization or fellow workers

8. If the "small talk" seems to be heading toward more serious or complicated subjects suggest that the discussion move to your office

9. With words, inflection, and body language indicate your interest in the person and the topic you are discussing. There are other ways to act that will make you approachable by your subordinates and colleagues alike. These might include:

    a. Be relaxed and not rushed, be enthusiastic, and show enjoyment for the chance to "chitchat" with a fellow worker

    b. Be "other person" centered

    c. Be responsive with questions and add to the conversation

    d. Don't abruptly change the subject

    e. Give the person and the topic full attention; do not appear preoccupied

    f. Be sincere as you participate; don't just "go through the motions"

g. Base your reactions and your comments on whom you're talking with; equal, subordinate, or superior

h. Let the conversation end naturally. However, it is certainly okay to end the chat if necessary

i. Be friendly, natural, and genuine during the conversation but be careful not to make comments or express an opinion that could cause you problems

10. Remember, that although informal and unscheduled, the "small talk" is a very important means of communicating inside and outside the organization. As a manager you must be aware of how to use this method to keep informed, show your interest in your subordinates, and collegiality among your peers.

Offering Employees Credit for Their Achievements

"If we are deprived of our just due, we naturally experience emotions of anger"

—DrSmiley Blanton

A. Things to Know and B. Things to Do

- Be sure to give credit to your subordinates whenever they deserve it. Give credit promptly and enthusiastically.
- Giving credit at appropriate times motivates employees and shows you notice and appreciate their efforts.
- It is extremely important that, as a manager, you never take credit for what your subordinates do. However, it is okay to share the credit when it is appropriate to do so.
- You will be wise and viewed more favorably when you downplay your own achievements and emphasize those of your subordinates.
- There are three steps to take when giving employees credit:
  1. Be aware of the times when credit is due. Start by stating specifically what the employee did that warrants special recognition.
  - Extend the credit promptly while maintaining steady eye contact and speaking in a lively manner and with a happy facial expression.
  - Place information about the achievement in the person's personnel record if sufficiently important
  2. Explain why the achievement was so noteworthy
  - Tell the person how his/her achievement benefits the organization, the work unit and you as manager. Emphasize the importance of the accomplishment by your use of powerful words and not rushing your comments.
  3. Demonstrate by words, voice tone, and body action how much you appreciate the employee's contribution

- Thank the employee sincerely and after a brief expression of your gratitude, say something such as "keep up the good work" as you shake hands and end the conversation.
- Notify the employees throughout the organization of the person's achievement by the organization's newsletter or employee bulletin.

One final point—you can get a lot done if you don't worry about who gets the credit for something well done.

TOPIC 21

Giving and Receiving Praise Comfortably

*"The deepest principle of human nature is the craving
to be appreciated"*

—William James

1. Giving Praise:

A. Things to Know

- Praise is one of the best and one of the least expensive rewards any manager has available to encourage and recognize excellent performance.
- Managers need to realize that failing to criticize an employee does not equal the granting of praise.
- Regrettably too many managers are both uncomfortable and unskilled in their well-intended endeavors to compliment their employees.
- The message is clear—if an employee does something well managers should say so.
- Lack of appreciation turns people off. Most employees want recognition in return for their good work. If they don't get it they become discouraged and feel used.
- As a manager you don't have to go around patting everyone on the back to show your appreciation, but you do need to note what employees do well and show you appreciate it.
- People are especially responsive to unexpected compliments and unsolicited praise because they appear to be the most sincere.
- If you conscientiously avoid giving superficial praise or the use of praise for ulterior reasons, your credibility will increase.
- Act comfortable and enthusiastic when praising people.

- Offer praise only when deserved and don't make the mistake of praising excessively. If you praise excessively the praise will lose its affect. Also avoid offering false praise in an attempt to manipulate—this causes resentment.
- Specific praise means the most and is remembered the longest by employees (merely saying "good job" isn't good enough).
- Avoid mixed message compliments, focus only on the compliment and don't add anything negative.
- Most employees find flattering statements not only embarrassing but useless (they also create suspicion).

B. *Things to Do*

- Look for opportunities to extend praise when an employee does something noteworthy.
- Select the most appropriate time and situation for sharing an especially deserved compliment. Optimal timing and the proper setting are important whether the praise is given privately or publicly.
- Use the employee's name when praising him/her and adapt the way you do the praising to the employee's personality.
- Make the compliments specific and tangible. For example, "Sharon your speech was excellent, I particularly enjoyed your comments on cost containment."
- Be enthusiastic and show you like giving people earned praise.
- Know when it is most appropriate to praise publicly or privately (public commendation can also serve to motivate other employees).
- Sometimes it is best to be indirect when praising shy people. For example, you could ask for their advice or for the employee to assist you on an important project.
- Take your time and act comfortable when praising employees.
- Compliment employees promptly—don't wait too long or the compliment will lose its value.
- Inform employees about favorable things you have heard about their work from people important to them.

- Share compliments not only with the employee but with significant others in his/her life. For example, the family.
- Follow up verbal compliments on important matters with a written statement for the employee's personnel file.
- When praising employees there are several things you should avoid doing:
  1. Avoid embarrassing the person you are praising
  2. Don't act uncomfortable or embarrassed when giving praise because this makes the receiver feel ill at ease
  3. Avoid rushing the compliment or acting as if you can't wait to get it over with
  4. Don't give praise begrudgingly or damn with faint praise
  5. Look the employee in the eyes with a smile on your face while rendering the compliment
  6. Don't patronize or act superior when commending an employee
  7. Avoid superficial praise or flattery
  8. Don't use praise as a type of sarcasm or ridicule. For example "Jim, good going, it's nice to see that you got your report in on time for once"
  9. Remember Mark Twain's famous quotation on the importance of praise "I can live for two months on a good compliment"
  10. Offering praise in the proper way makes the employee feel worthwhile and like a somebody and we all like to feel like a somebody

2. Receiving Praise:

A. Things to Know

- It is important to act composed, assured, and modest when being praised
- Employees who fail to accept praise graciously make the person offering the praise feel uncomfortable and cause the manager extending the praise to be reluctant to praise people in the future
- Accepting praise graciously involves verbal and nonverbal reactions that convey appreciation

- Managers become reluctant to praise people who react negatively or appear embarrassed when being complimented
- Employees should act appreciative and modest while receiving compliments
- Employees should avoid fishing for compliments as this is in poor taste and puts managers in an awkward position
- People should accept the praise graciously and make only a brief response while accepting the praise
- Receivers of praise need to be careful that they don't say anything trite or anything that belittles what the person praising has said. Above all, don't dismiss the praise abruptly as being unwarranted
- Statements such as these are effective when accepting praise:
  1. "Thank you."
  2. "Thank you. I'm pleased that you liked my presentation."
  3. "Thank you. I'm glad you liked my report because I worked hard on it."
  4. "Thank you. I appreciate your comments and they make me feel really good."
  5. "Thank you. I was happy to be able to help."
- Conversely, avoid these kinds of reactions when accepting praise:
  1. "Oh that, there was nothing to it. You must be kidding."
  2. "I'm surprised to hear you say you liked my report because I don't think I wrote the report well at all."
  3. "It was really nothing—anyone could have done it."
  4. "Thank you but I don't know why you are complimenting me because I didn't do anything special."
  5. "I was wondering when you were going to say something because I think I did an exceptionally good job on the project."

TOPIC 22

Thinking Before Speaking To Say What You Mean

"It is necessary to think before speaking but you must also think while speaking"

—Kenneth McFarland

A. Things to Know and B. Things to Do

- Think before you speak or write
- Think ahead about the possible consequences or your message before saying or writing anything
- Spur of the moment statements without the benefit of clear and careful thought can easily cause problems and can even be dangerous
- Although trite, there is a lot of wisdom in this caution "Put your mind in gear before you put your mouth in motion"
- Clear thinking must precede clear expression
- Clear thinking doesn't just happen—it requires strong mental discipline
- Clear thinking involves an organized, systematic, logical, and objective thought process. Clear statements are free of ambiguity, fuzziness, and confusion.
- You will benefit from considering these factors before you say anything important:
  1. Have a clear and specific purpose before you communicate anything
  2. Identify the person or target group to receive your message
  3. Think before you say anything and also while you are saying it
  4. Assess your own attitude and your receiver's attitude toward the subject and the contents of your message before sending it
  5. Think about your personal relationship with the people you are communicating with

6. Figure out the best method and time to send your message

7. Create a strategy that will make the message appeal to your receivers—show at the beginning of the message how the message will benefit them personally (answer "What's in it for me?" for the people receiving the message)

8. Make sure that the words you plan to use are compatible with things you have said in the past as well as your previous actions

9. Be aware that your current health condition and mood may significantly affect what you plan to say and how you say it

10. Adapt the wording and content of your message to the interests, intelligence, and knowledge of the receivers of your communication

11. Make a concerted effort to word your message clearly by using common, familiar, and simple words (avoid using words with multiple meanings)

12. Organize what you plan to say in a logical way with definite transitions for the different points you plan to present

13. Think about how your message can have greater impact by including both impressive facts and emotional statements

- Clear important communications with your boss if your relationship with him/her or the organizational climate makes this advisable

- It is wise to ask yourself these questions before sending a message:

  1. What would be the best and worst things that could happen if I said what I would like to say frankly?

  2. What would happen if I didn't say exactly what I would like to say?

  3. How can I say what I intend to say to get the best results.

  4. Should I say what I need to say now or delay saying it until a more opportune time.

Personal Qualities Managers Need to Communicate Effectively

Positive Attitudes and Beliefs

"Trust that man in nothing who has not a conscience on everything"
—Lawrence Stern

A. Things to Know and Things to Do

1. Attitudes

- Attitude is a mental position or feeling about something. If you can't see something being done it is attitude, if you see something being done it is behavior.
- It is helpful to view attitude in four contexts:
  1. One's self-perception
  2. Manager's views toward people
  3. Manager's attitude toward work
  4. Manager's attitude about communicating on-the-job
- You are responsible for your own attitudes and beliefs. Your attitude determines your behavior. On the other hand, when new behavior becomes habitual it can change your attitude.
- Your attitude is the foundation of your relationship with people. It determines how you act, what you say, and how you say things to people.
- You need to control your attitudes because they can cause problems for you and the organization. Also, your attitudes

determine whether you succeed or fail at your job (and also in life).

- Unfortunately, communications research consistently shows that there is a wide disparity between how a manager's attitude and behavior are perceived by the manager compared with how they are viewed by his/her employees.
- Many managers pride themselves on communicating impersonally and objectively with employees, whereas most employees prefer to be communicated with on a more personal basis.

1. Manager's attitude toward him/herself and his/her own conduct
   - Know and accept who you are
   - Like yourself and have a positive self-esteem
   - Feel relaxed and at ease with yourself
   - Be open-minded, adaptable, and flexible
   - Have convictions and principles that guide your thinking
   - Have a cheerful and upbeat disposition
   - Maintain a positive and optimistic view of life
   - Accept the fact that as a human you are not perfect and will make mistakes
   - Feel competent, confident, and self-assured
   - View authority as service to people rather than power over them
   - Be willing to act real and natural
   - Have the courage to be candid and be willing to reveal rather than conceal
   - Have a modest mental set and one that emphasizes "oh there you are" instead of . . ."well here I am" when greeting someone
   - Be willing to say "I don't know" when you don't know something
   - Desire to keep your promises, honor commitments, and follow up on things
   - Be wise enough to know what can and can't be changed and accept this without feeling resentment
   - Have a positive regard for others by feeling "I'm okay," "you are okay," and that "we are okay" when reacting with people
   - Do the best you can and realize you can't please all of the people all of the time

2. Recommended manager's attitudes toward people
   - Be willing to treat people as they want to be treated rather than as you want to be treated
   - Desire to treat people, with respect, politeness, and patience
   - Stress YOU (be other-centered) and minimize I (being self-centered)
   - Want to be responsive and to help people whenever they need to be helped instead of only when it is convenient for you
   - Try to make people feel safe and secure with you instead of feeling insecure and defensive
   - Be nonjudgmental toward other people's thinking and acting
   - Be sensitive to the needs of culturally diverse people, older, and disabled employees
   - View all racial and ethnic groups as equals
   - Be willing to communicate at distances (spaces) the other person is comfortable with
   - Strive to be comfortable with and to like all employees (show no favoritism)
   - Desire to be friendly, kind, and compassionate when interacting with people
   - Strive to learn employee's names and the "little things" about them (for example their nicknames and hobbies)
   - Trust people and strive to be trusted by them
   - Realize people have feelings that are important to them and that you need to deal with them rather than simply dismissing them
   - Try to achieve a sense of commonality and togetherness as coworkers
   - Have the attitude that it is what is right that is important rather than who is right over something
   - Be genuinely interested in the welfare of all employees, their work, their achievements, and their problems
   - Be readily available to employees (both approachable and accessible)
   - View employees as people with dignity who are important and valuable both as individuals and employees

3. Important manager's attitudes about work and the work climate
   - Minimize status and role differences and treat employees as equal human beings
   - Know and accept your responsibilities, but be willing to delegate freely
   - Emphasize the desire for excellence rather than being willing to accept "good enough" as a work standard
   - Allow employees to be meaningfully involved in matters affecting them
   - Promote the employees' feelings of having the freedom and independence to do their job
   - Be interested in both the employee and his/her work
   - Strive to understand the employee's job: its duties, its demands, pressures, problems, and accompanying frustrations
   - Be enthusiastic when doing and talking about your job
   - Be an opportunity seeker rather than a problem finder concerning your work
   - Offer help when it is needed, but avoid being controlling
   - Be willing to compromise when negotiating something
   - Allow employees to express respectful disagreeing with you on work-related problems
   - Avoid engaging in one-upmanship or taking all the credit for the work unit achievements
   - Be willing to provide support in difficult situations and in uncertain times
   - Strive to follow up on matters and seek prompt closure
   - Be alert to opportunities to express appreciation to employees
   - Try to be open-minded, objective, and nonjudgmental
   - Have a can do, let's try it, attitude—respond to suggestions with receptive remarks such as "Let's see, how could we make your idea work?" rather than negatively with reactions such as this: "Your idea is too risky" or "It won't work—we tried it before."
4. Recommended manager's attitudes aiding communicating
   - Strive to develop mutual perceptions of people, things, and events

- Realize that when you communicate it is not only for today but for tomorrow
- Know that your personality affects your communications immensely
- Be willing to adapt your communicating style to the people you are talking with, the topic, and the situation
- Think carefully before saying, writing, or doing anything
- Learn what your specific communicating strengths and weaknesses are
- Have the courage to level with people and to say it as it is without being insulting
- Realize that how you say something is at least as important as what you are saying
- Desire to communicate and be communicated with
- Be a patient listener, hear people out, don't make assumptions, premature judgments, or jump to conclusions
- View and communicate with people as an equal—avoid acting superior, condescending, and holier than thou
- Strive to understand as well as to get understood
- Strive to communicate simply and to express rather than to impress
- Recognize that communication is two-way (a sender sends a message and a receiver responds to the message)
- Understand that touch is the most important of all communications techniques but needs to be done in the right way at the right time
- Try to create a climate conducive to candid and relaxed communication
- Honor confidences and protect confidential and proprietary information
- Be willing to listen attentively, patiently, and with an open mind
- Give communication a top priority and be sure to give it sufficient time
- Maintain an open-door policy and more importantly wander around outside of your office and among your employees regularly

- Strive to share information with employees promptly
- Identify the informal leaders and opinion molders throughout the organization and be sure to communicate with them regularly
- Realize the importance of maintaining an effective pipeline to enable you to receive information informally
- Try to maintain open and fast communications channels in all directions

5. Recommended communications beliefs for managers
   - A person has a belief when he/she has a mental conviction or acceptance of something as true or actual
   - Management needs to develop a set of important communications beliefs and to use them as a framework for the organization's communications philosophy and policies
   - These beliefs need to be listed in the Employee's Handbook and discussed during new employee orientation
   - Here are several important communications beliefs of managers:
     1. That management considers an effective communications program or system to be essential for the entire organization
     2. That management fully backs and supports the communications program
     3. That management believes that employees share the responsibility for maintaining an effective communications program
     4. That management endorses employee communications rights and will honor them
     5. That each manager and employee should actively promote a healthy communications climates organization-wide
     6. That management considers all employee ideas, suggestions, and complaints to be important and pledges to respond to them promptly
     7. That management recognizes the importance of two-way communication and commits to excellent upward as well as downward communication
     8. That management will try to communicate vital information to employees on a right-to-know rather than a need-to-know basis

9. That employees receive a full explanation, including reasons, about all important decisions and actions affecting their jobs and future with the organization
10. That management will keep all employees informed of their performance so they will always know where they stand and how they are doing
11. That management intends to share both good and bad news to employees in a forthright manner
12. That management's main concern and guide for all of the communications program is this question: "are we getting through to our people effectively and are they able to get through to us effectively?"

TOPIC 24

Realistic Expectations

"The quality of our expectations determine the quality of our actions"
—André Godin

A. Things to Know and Things to Do

1. Expectations of Managers:

- The manager's communications expectations of his/her subordinates need to be reasonable and realistic
- The following list presents the manager's most important expectations:
    1. Employees ongoing comments should express their loyalty to the organization and management
    2. Employees promptly inform management of any dangerous hazards or unsanitary conditions that could endanger the workforce
    3. Employees attitudes, actions, and utterances should promote a healthy communications climate
    4. Employees have ideas and suggestions for doing things better, faster, and cheaper
    5. Employees air opposition to proposed changes frankly and openly to management
    6. Employees readily admit it when they don't know something rather than bluff or guess at answers
    7. Employees keep management informed of progress, problems, or deviations from approved plans
    8. Employees secure permission in advance to do something important that is new before taking action
    9. Employees should be open-minded and receptive to management's communications and do their best to understand them
    10. Employees need to furnish prompt feedback to managers to verify that they understand a message or need to have it clarified

11. Employees communicate at the best times for managers as much as possible

12. Employees get right to the point and stick to it when conferring with managers

13. Employees communicate proactively when they have a problem or need something

14. Employees should feel free to disagree with managers in a sincere, respectful, and tactful manner

15. Employees who strongly oppose something managers say, or what managers want, should do it privately to avoid embarrassing the manager and causing tension

16. Employees should provide managers with face-saving comments in public rather than criticisms that make them look bad

17. Employees are expected to safeguard confidential information

18. Employees are expected to follow up on manager's suggestions, criticism, and requests

2. Expectations of Employees:

- Managers explain the chain of command and reporting relationship clearly
- Employees want managers to keep them informed regularly and to share bad news as well as good news candidly
- Managers share information on goals, priorities, performance standards and criteria, and the amount of freedom and authority employees have to do their jobs
- Managers let them know the resources and assistance that are available to help them with their work
- Managers keep employees promptly and fully informed of changes and other matters that will affect their work
- Managers point out their specific performance strengths and weaknesses during their performance evaluation and jointly develop a plan to overcome the weaknesses
- Managers offer continuous feedback on how the employee is doing and where he/she stands
- Managers keep employees informed of professional development (training) opportunities for them

- Managers show interest in them as a person as well as their work
- Managers know their names and pronounce their names correctly
- Managers know what jobs they have and the duties and problems involved in performing their job
- Managers provide employees clear, in-depth instructions on how to do their jobs, without being controlling
- Managers listen to employees' ideas and suggestions with interest and open minds and respond to them within a reasonable length of time
- Managers provide a system for employees to share their frustrations and air their complaints without recrimination
- Managers express their appreciation for employee accomplishments freely and in an appropriate manner
- Managers criticize and reprimand them privately at the appropriate time without overkill
- Managers use plain, simple, easy to understand language when talking with them
- Managers treat employees fairly, not equally, when interacting with them since all people are not equal, or the same, and consequently need to be dealt with differently to be fair
- Managers consider employee requests carefully and if they need to deny them explain the reasons for doing so
- Managers offer their support and encouragement to employees in rough and uncertain times
- Managers listen to employee's feelings as well as the facts when discussing a matter that is serious and upsets them
- Managers keep upward communication channels open and unclogged to allow for speedy unfiltered transmission of information
- Managers protect confidences shared with them by their subordinates
- Managers explain the security arrangements and requirements
- Managers describe accident procedures and the location of first aid supplies

TOPIC 25

Ethical Standards

"Never promise more than you can perform"
—Publilius Syrus

1. Manager as a Communicator

A. Things to Know

- .There is no right way to do the wrong thing
- Ethics may be defined as approved or acceptable principles or standards of conduct by an individual or group such as a profession
- We shall offer seven categories of standards to guide managers: (1) manager as a communicator, (2) manager as a listener, (3) information to share with employees, (4) communication methods managers use, (5) managers use of communication channels, (6) managers timing of messages, (7) and managers unethical communicating behavior.
- Be aware of, and make employees aware of, their communications rights and responsibilities
- View communication as a service to employees rather having power over them
- Remain silent when it is in the best interests of all involved parties
- Managers are ethically obligated to be reasonably available to their employees. Availability has two dimensions: approachability and accessibility
- Managers are responsible for respecting and safeguarding their subordinate's rights to privacy and confidentiality of their personal information

B. Things to Do

- Managers are expected to actively support and faithfully follow the organization's goals, policies, and procedures as well as the provisions set forth in the union contact re: communication
- Manager's actions should be consistent with their words (they should actually do what they say they are going to do)
- Managers should speak truthfully to their employees (they should say what they mean and mean what they say)
- Managers should say, "I don't know" when they really don't know the answer to a question rather than replying by guessing, bluffing, or lying
- Managers should treat and communicate the way employees want to be treated and communicated with and not the way they (managers) want to be treated and communicated with
- Managers should let employees know what is expected of them, how they are doing, and where they stand
- Managers need to provide a private place to discuss sensitive and confidential matters with their employees
- Managers should sincerely welcome and duly consider all of their employees' ideas and suggestions and then respond to them within a reasonable length of time
- Managers should routinely request employee input and feedback on matters affecting their work
- Managers need to restrict their questions of employees to work-related and noninvasive kinds of questions
- Managers should ask only fair worded or neutral worded questions instead of loaded, leading, and slanted questions
- Managers need to use gender fair or sex neutral language when communicating with employees
- Managers should use appropriate and socially acceptable words and language (this does not mean they need to feel compelled to use politically correct language)
- Managers should use "I statements" to accept responsibility and ownership for their own statements and actions. Conversely, they should not use "they statements" to avoid the responsibility that can accompany the risk of making "I statements"

- Managers should explain their reasons for making decisions and taking action on matters affecting their employee's job and their working conditions
- Managers are advised to level with their employees when necessary but to do it as tactful as possible
- Managers need to disagree agreeably and to object without being objectionable
- Managers need to treat an employee as a person, compassionately, but the facts objectively when discussing a problem with an employee

2. The Manager as a Listener:

A. Things to Know:

- Please note that listening skills are discussed in detail in a separate section of this book

B. Things to Do

- Look interested and act attentive to everything an employee is saying to you while discussing anything important and avoid saying or doing anything to make the employee feel rushed
- Seek to understand what your employees are saying to you as much as you want them to understand what you are saying to them
- Hear employees out rather than interrupting, prejudging, and jumping to conclusions re: what they are saying
- Interrupt people only to seek clarification about something they are saying
- Listen to employee statements with a receptive and open mind
- Concentrate on what an employee is saying to you instead of being preoccupied with what you want to say next

3. Information to Share with Employees:

A. Things to Know and Things to Do:

- Disseminate information to employees that is specific, clear, complete, current, correct, concise, and reliable

- Provide all new employees with a comprehensive orientation and a copy of the Employee Handbook the day they begin work
- Inform employees of their communications rights and responsibilities their first day on the job
- Make certain that the information system is driven by the needs of the organization and its employees
- Transmit factual, current, objective, and balanced information
- Explain the communications expectations of employees when they start work and the penalties if they are not met
- Emphasize that employees should not air the organization's problems and "dirty linen" in public
- Share appropriate news concerning the organization to the public and news media in a timely fashion
- Share the reasons for important decisions and changes with employees in an appropriate and timely manner
- Administer employee opinion surveys as advisable and share the complete results with employees soon after they are tabulated
- Communicate both good and bad news candidly with employees on a timely basis
- Refrain from both initiating and spreading rumors
- Encourage managers to speak out on important matters rather than remaining silent when it is imperative that the news become known
- Identify and make known the nature of confidential information to employees
- Protect all confidential and proprietary information
- Develop a policy and follow all laws pertaining to retention of records
- Tell employees what you honestly think about important matters, and what they need to know, instead of telling them what they want to hear

4. Communications Methods Managers Use

A. Things to Know:

- Please note that methods (media) is covered in detail in a separate section of the book

B. Things to Do

- Convey all information in a candid straightforward manner
- Share important, complicated, and detailed information both verbally and in writing
- Share bad and sensitive information face-to-face
- Select the methods that are the most direct and fastest because they permit the least amount of filtering and distortion of meaning
- Include all the people in a meeting who can contribute something or who will be affected by the meeting content—exclude everyone else
- Separate the content of a message from the messenger. The important thing is what is being said not who is saying it
- Use tele and video conferencing to advantage and be sure to identify all participants, and strive to keep their comments relevant and brief
- Select the type of method to use based on content and timing factors
- Go to employees to obtain information you need instead of waiting for them to come to you with it—be proactive

5. *Managers Use of Communications Channels*

A. Things to Know and Things to Do:

- All employees should have equal access to the communications channels
- Channels should flow quickly in both directions—upward and downward
- Official channels must be known and followed by employees. Bypassing or circumventing of channels should be prohibited except for emergencies
- The only times and situations when it is okay to bypass channels should be publicized and known to all employees
- Upward communicating should be as fast and easy as downward communication
- Employees originating or actively engaged in spreading rumors should be severely disciplined

6. *Managers Timing of Messages*

A. Things to Know and Things to Do:

- There is a right and a wrong time to say, to hear, and to do anything
- Communicate in a timely manner
- Give employees sufficient advance notice—the more important the information the more advance notice should be given
- Communicate regularly and on an ongoing basis rather than infrequently and sporadically
- Managers and employees should keep each other informed re: problems promptly
- Follow up on employee suggestions, requests, and complaints promptly or explain why there is a delay
- Send copies of meeting minutes to appropriate people within three working days following the meeting
- Communicate important news to employees before releasing it to the general public
- Share appropriate news with the news media at the proper time
- Be aware of media deadlines when releasing information
- Insist that employees refrain from sending messages of a personal nature or viewing television or the Internet during working hours without the prior approval of their supervisor
- Managers should be available to discuss employee problems within a reasonable time

7. *Managers Unethical Communications Behaviors*

A. Things to Know and Things to Do:

- Creating and spreading malicious rumors
- Providing a misleading or false image when communicating
- Being insincere, saying or doing one thing, and believing or doing the opposite

- Sharing slanted, biased, partial, and unreliable information
- Asking loaded or leading questions to trap people
- Answering a question with so many qualifying words that you leave yourself an out but fail to answer the question
- Sacrificing your convictions on an important issue in order to win agreement on the matter under discussion
- Doctoring or misrepresenting the facts in order to gain support for your ideas or proposals
- Plagiarism
- Using an emotional appeal to gain support for your position when there are no facts or evidence to give credence to your position or proposal
- Offering unfair, unbalance, and biased information in an effort to win over the opposition to make your case (strive to be ethical in all that you say and do)

TOPIC 26

Winning Style of Communicating

"A man's natural manner best becomes him"

—Cicero

A. Things to Know

- There is no one best style for communicating with all people in all situations
- People usually have a blended style of communicating, but they also have a dominant or primary style of communicating
- People generally change their style of communicating depending on the relationship they have with the person they are talking with and the particular situation
- People are free to choose how they want to communicate with others
- People reflect their communications styles by the way they send and receive information
- People show their primary style by what they say and how they say it
- One of the worst communications styles is the manipulative one because it diminishes and antagonizes people
- People communicate best with people who think and act like they do
- People with an effective communication style analyze and adapt to other people's way of communicating
- People need to avoid acting impatient, interrupting others' comments, making hasty assumptions, pre-judging what is said, and jumping to conclusions
- People need to know when to push the off button when listening to logic and facts and start to listen to peoples' feelings when discussing important personal matters

- Self-centered people care more about their needs and agenda than the needs and concerns of the people they are talking with
- People's personality has a significant influence
  1. It is important for managers to know how their personality is perceived by their employees because their personality has a strong effect on their ability to communicate. It is unrealistic to expect managers to make major changes in their personality. However, it is realistic for managers to modify their attitudes and behavior in order for them to communicate better with their coworkers.
  2. Managers' choices affecting their communications style Managers can make several choices of attitude and behavior that will significantly affect their communications style and ability to communicate with people
- Here are several of the most important choices available to managers
- Prefer face-to-face communication over written
- Favor being open and approachable to being reserved and aloof
- Be primarily a listener rather than a talker
- Maintain an open-door policy instead of meeting only by appointment
- Prefer to communicate on a right-to-know basis rather than a need-to-know basis
- Desire to say things as they are as opposed to being politically correct
- Reveal real feelings about an issue rather than concealing them
- Concentrate on both the facts and feelings connected to an issue rather than only the facts
- Prefer to get background information about a problem first on some issues, but for others prefer to obtain bottom-line information first
- Prefer to be an idea guy first and a details person second
- State things frankly regardless of the consequences instead of toning down statements to play it safe
- prefer getting directly to the point rather than engaging in small talk before discussing a problem
- Be other person-centered rather than self-centered when talking with employees

- Have convictions and a set of principles that guide your thoughts and actions rather than making decisions based solely on the particular situation
- Use plain and simple language when communicating with employees instead of using fancy language
- Be willing to adapt your communications style to other people's rather than expecting them to adapt to yours
- Be comfortable with being disagreed with rather than feeling resentful and intimidated

B. Things to Do

You can improve your communicating style and gain valuable insights into your style by asking yourself these kinds of questions:

- Do I communicate from a win-win position?
- Is what I want to communicate consistently more important to me than what others want to discuss?
- Do I try to understand other people's viewpoints?
- Does whether or not I like a person affect how I talk and listen to him/her?
- Am I biased in my opinion of certain other groups and does this affect how I treat them?
- Am I basically a positive or negative thinker?
- Do I listen objectively to and accept criticism or do I ignore and resent it?
- Do I welcome or resent other peoples' ideas and suggestions?
- Do I respect and show respect for the ideas and viewpoints of people that I disagree with?
- Do I know what my employees think of me and how I communicate?
- Am I content to be what I am or am I willing to change to meet other people's expectations of me?
- Do I understand that my personality influences all of my on-the-job relationships and communications?
- Do I have enough interest and courage to ask informed people for feedback about my communications style?
- Am I willing to change my communications style based on constructive feedback?

SECTION 5

TOPIC 27

Communicating and Relating Strategies for Safeguarding the Manager's Job

"A man sir, should keep his friendship in constant repair"

—Samuel Johnson

A. Things to Know and Things to Do

1. Before Accepting the Job Activity:

- The first steps in safeguarding your job begin before you accept the job
- It is imperative that you consider how well you and the job match up. Find out all you can about the reputation and operation of the organization as well as the position you are applying for. You can acquire this information by:
  1. Talking with employees
  2. Chatting with people living in the community
  3. Asking the interviewer relevant questions
  4. Examining the employee handbook, newsletters, and annual report
- It is imperative that you get as much job protection language in your contract as is fair and reasonable
- Keep your attempts to learn about the job and organization low key and discreet to avoid alienating management and jeopardizing your job offer

2. Recommended Attitude for Managers:

- Having and displaying the proper attitude is crucial to the success of managers. Recommended attitudes include:
  1. Liking and respecting yourself and other people
  2. Feeling confident and secure yet acting modest
  3. Being realistic, reasonable, and fair minded
  4. Possessing a positive and optimistic outlook toward work and life
- Being friendly, considerate, and approachable
- Expecting effective performance by employees
- Expecting employees to make mistakes occasionally
- Refraining from being overly ambitious and pushy career wise
- Being willing to lose sometimes without resenting it or holding grudges
- Emphasizing what is right, not who is right when disagreeing
- Encouraging ideas and suggestions from employees instead of being an idea killer

3. Managers Cautions Re: Comments:

- Be careful with what you say, how you say it, when you say it, and who you say it to
- Words are like bullets—once said they cannot be recalled
- People may forgive improper or offensive comments but they never forget them
- Here are some cautions managers should observe about things they should say and avoid saying before saying anything:
  1. Think and consider the consequences before saying anything important or sensitive—avoid making spur-of-the-moment comments on significant matters
  2. Analyze the situation and the people involved before saying anything of consequence
  3. Know when it is best to talk and when it is best to remain silent
  4. Use we and you often and I, me, my as little as possible when conversing
  5. Say the right thing, in the right way at the right time

6. Use appropriate language. Avoid profanity, inflammatory, and insulting language

7. Be especially careful about what you say to and about individuals and groups belonging to protected classes

8. Strive to avoid making any sexist remarks

9. Refrain from speaking ill of coworkers and other work units

10. Be positive when communicating. Don't use demeaning, condescending, or put down words

11. Avoid frequent or habitual complaining and griping

12. Say it as it is. Level with people and remember to be diplomatic when doing so

13. Resist the temptation to be evasive, bluff, or guess when answering questions from your employees

14. Avoid being euphemistic or politically correct when the situation demands sincere and straightforward talk

15. Never represent opinions as facts

16. Talk with employees not at them

17. Disagree with employees agreeably rather than coming on like gangbusters and overwhelming them with an excessive defense of your position on a mater

18. Make objective comments and do your best not to make judgmental and biased comments habitually

19. Speak for tomorrow as well as for today

4. Essential Communications Knowledge and Skills for Managers:

- Communications is at the heart of the management process. Successful mangers know how to communicate effectively. These tips should help managers to improve their communications competency:

    1. Keep key people informed and communicate proactively

    2. Provide people with advanced notice. Make sure information reaches employees when they need it

    3. Consider people's moods and the situation before communicating anything important that isn't urgent.

4. Space and coordinate important information rather than sending several messages at one time

5. Use plain words and simple language

6. Express yourself briefly and clearly—don't confuse people by using big words and long complicated sentences

7. Be certain that your voice tone, word choices, and body language are consistent and send the same message (avoid sending mixed or contradictory messages)

8. Use the words that say what you intend to say—avoid using words in such a self-protective qualifying manner that they actually say nothing

9. Secure feedback on all vital matters to ensure that you have been understood or understand the message you have received

10. Speak loud enough to be understood easily

11. Speak less and listen more (listen to understand not to refute)

12. Listen attentively and hear people out without interrupting, jumping to conclusions, or pre-judging

13. When you have nothing good to say, it is best to say nothing

14. Avoid speculating, when answering employee's questions

15. Screen and proofread all outgoing messages (and screen all incoming messages)

16. Make sure your words and actions match (always keep your word)

17. Pause at appropriate times while speaking to encourage comments and questions from the people you are talking with

18. Read all important communications from important people promptly and carefully

19. Be responsive to what people say to you but be politely non-committal when you don't know something or you can't divulge confidential information—when appropriate cite the reasons you can't comment at the time

20. Protect confidence, confidential information, and proprietary information diligently

21. Keep your guard up when saying things to the news media or a rival organization

22. Pin down the content and sources of rumors and deal with them promptly if they are causing problems
23. Develop reliable pipelines and keep tuned into the grapevine
24. Communicate through official channels and resist the temptation to bypass people who are in the communications chain
25. Keep on top of important matters

5. Methods for Fitting into the Organization's Culture

- Study the organization's culture and do your best to accept the organization's philosophy, beliefs, and ways of doing things. However, beware of losing your own identity and compromising your own integrity and principles when doing so (this adjustment sometimes requires a delicate balancing act) if the organization expects you to fit into its culture smoothly
- These ideas will help you to fit in:
  1. Read the employee handbook and pay close attention at the organization's orientation sessions for new employees
  2. Ask your boss and other managers if there are any "unwritten rules" for the way to act and to do things that are important but aren't covered by the orientation or employee handbook (for example preferred ways of communicating)
  3. Dress appropriately for your job and be consistent with the organization's standards and expectations
  4. Make an impressive appearance, be well groomed, look fit, and present the desired image for a manager
  5. Keep a low profile and be a team player (emphasize we and us and de-emphasize I and me)
  6. Follow acceptable patterns of conduct and interacting
  7. Avoid having and sharing too many ideas and suggestions too soon that represent a significant change from the status quo or you may scare colleagues and create resentment
  8. Show your loyalty to the organization and speak highly of it both inside the organization and in the community whenever you get the chance

9. Keep from becoming controversial and championing unpopular causes
10. Learn as many names of coworkers in other departments as practical to develop rapport and to become "one of the guys"
11. Attend the organization's social functions and mix freely with your coworkers and their families
12. Furnish your office in good taste and appropriate for your rank in the organization (don't show up your fellow managers by having a fancy office)
13. Follow this time-honored advice "you've got to go along to get along"—unless doing so would violate your principles and jeopardize your integrity

6. Essential Performance Factors:

- There are numerous performance factors involved in determining a manager's success or failure. An entire book could be written about these factors alone. However, we shall endeavor to list only those that we consider to be the most important:
  1. Has clear and specific annual goals with priorities and action plans as well as an up-to-date accurate job description
  2. Accepts full responsibility for achieving the goals
  3. Performs duties willingly and competently
  4. Understands the type and extent of his/her authority and doesn't exceed it
  5. Works by priorities rather than being preoccupied with urgent but less important matters
  6. Maintains things to do check lists, target dates, and deadlines for all important projects
  7. Takes charge, gets things done promptly, deals with problems proactively, meets deadlines, and gets closure
  8. Puts in a long and productive day—works both harder and smarter
  9. Uses time wisely and productively
  10. Keeps informed and up-to-date on all matters related to his/her job

11. Secures his/her bosses approval before making important changes and is careful not to make too many changes too fast

12. Reports progress, problems, and deviations from plan to his/her boss and other people affected

13. Goes the extra mile to help his/her employees

14. Floats a trial balloon before taking action on something important or controversial to get reactions from affected parties

15. Checks with the organization's legal counsel, the Human Resources Department, and his/her boss before making important personnel decisions (in a union environment the union representative should also be appropriately involved and the union contract adhered to)

16. Have another manager present as a witness for certain types of disciplinary, evaluation, and dismissal sessions as deemed advisable

17. Develop a network of associates both on- and off-site

18. Know and understand the legal requirements, organization's policies, and union contract provisions that relate to your job

19. Work on a policy basis as much as possible

20. Develop a realistic budget (not padded) and allocate resources based on their importance (administer the budget carefully and follow recommended protocol)

21. Maintain proper records as this is an imperative for managers. These practices are recommended:

- Put important decisions and actions in writing and keep them in a secure place
- Be especially careful to safeguard confidential information
- Be careful who you do and don't send copies of confidential information to
- Keep an accurate account of both your personal and your department's expenditures (especially bidding procedure, a major purchase and anything unusual)
- Keep a log of important incoming and outgoing daily phone calls, e-mails, and letters as well as meetings attended
- Ask for questionable requests to be put in writing for the record

- Keep a record of all complaints and grievances including dates received, dates dealt with, and action taken
- Maintain a list of all reports of: health hazards, dangerous conditions and materials, accidents, and safety or sanitation problems

The record should include date when report received, remedy sought, action taken, as well as all pertinent dates

7. Relations with Your Boss:

- Almost anyone who has a job has a boss to please. Your boss is very important to you because in many ways he/she controls your future
- There are many ways to please a boss. You will find these guidelines helpful in your efforts to develop and maintain a harmonious relationship with your boss:
  1. Learn everything you can about your boss—especially his/her likes and dislikes
  2. Find out what is important to your boss. Accept the fact that if your boss thinks something is important that it is also important to you so act accordingly
  3. Do everything you can to help your boss look good and succeed
  4. Be supportive, loyal and defend your boss' actions
  5. Refrain from saying anything critical or embarrassing about your boss or the organization
  6. Accept your boss' authority and never dispute it or undermine it
- Be a team player and never appear to be a threat to your boss or try to show him/her up
- Adapt to your boss' work style and preferred ways of doing things (for example know his/her preferred way to communicate and adjust your communications style to his/hers for best results)
- Think of ways to help your boss do his/her job faster, better, and easier
- Compensate for your boss's weaknesses with your strengths

- Know what your boss expects of you and provide it. It is a good idea to do your work according to your boss' priorities
- Gain agreement with your boss regarding your job goals and responsibilities, priorities, action plan, performance standards, and deadlines
- Meet deadlines and don't make excuses when you fail to meet them
- Anticipate problems with your work and try to prevent them or deal with them without needing your boss's help
- Share your ideas for solving problems when discussing them with the boss, but don't offer unsolicited advice if it is unwelcome or is likely to be resented
- Provide your boss with advanced notice on important matters and avoid surprising him/her on important things
- Keep your boss informed of your work unit's progress, problems, and deviations from plans
- Obtain approval in advance from the boss for something new or to make a major change, but don't seek unnecessary approval that consumes your boss's valuable time
- Be candid—don't try to hide anything from your boss
- Learn how to disagree with your boss without offending him/her or creating resentment
- Know what you can and can't disagree with your boss about and the times it is best to avoid disagreeing
- Disagree with your boss quietly, tactfully, and privately. Avoid engaging in one-upmanship and be alert to his/her need to save face
- You have a professional obligation to fight for what is right and to disagree about the right things in the right way to keep your boss from making a serious mistake
- Learn how and when to make suggestions or share bad news, complain, and present problems to the boss (when presenting a problem it is best to have a proposed solution at the same time, if possible)
- Be readily available to the boss. Keep your office assistant informed of your whereabouts, what you are doing, and when

you are due to return so he/she can tell the boss if he/she is trying to reach you

- Protect your boss's time
- Make appointments to discuss important matters and make a list of things you need to discuss. Anticipate possible questions from your boss and be ready with your answers
- Establish a feeling of commonality with your boss by sharing common interests (for example hobbies)
- Greet your boss at the start of every day and maintain ongoing contact without consuming too much of his/her time
- Get along with your coworkers and avoid conflict that would require your boss's involvement and need to take sides

8. Relations with Your Subordinates:

- Act human and treat subordinates as valuable fellow human beings
- Be both approachable and accessible
- Act relaxed and comfortable with subordinates
- Take and show a personal interest in your subordinates
- Promote subordinates' self-esteem by making them feel needed and important
- Respect the rights of your subordinates
- Help your subordinates to grow and reach their potential
- Know the strengths and weaknesses of your subordinates' performance
- Exude the attitude that your subordinates work with you— not for you
- Delegate duties to your subordinates frequently to show that you have confidence in them and trust them
- Minimize criticizing and faultfinding of subordinates
- Criticize and discipline employees privately after verifying that there is justification and cause
- Empower subordinates by involving them in appropriate planning, decision-making, and by being receptive to their suggestions

- Give praise and credit promptly when earned
- Respond to employee questions and requests promptly
- Keep subordinates informed of upcoming events, changes, and important activities well in advance
- Be helpful and perceived as such
- Strive for excellence rather than perfection in the performance of the work unit and employees
- Remember the "little things" that are so important to employees (the little things are actually big things to employees)
- Get feedback to verify that you have understood your employees and that they have understood you
- Level with your employees without leveling them in the process
- Greet employees at the start of the work day and wish them well
- Show your subordinates that you understand their problems and compliment them when they go the extra mile on a project
- Be polite, remember the niceties, and say please and thank you often
- Give subordinates an opportunity to tell their story after making a mistake or causing a problem
- Be calm and even-tempered when discussing a big mistake by a subordinate
- Let your subordinates get their way on an issue sometimes even though, as a manager, you have the authority to get your way on the issue
- Treat all employees fairly and avoid having favorites or showing favoritism
- Apologize to subordinates sincerely and graciously when it is deserved—don't wait too long to apologize or the apology will lose its impact
- Provide a healthy and pleasant work climate
- Form a group of representative subordinates to meet with you monthly, quarterly or whenever needed to discuss their

concerns, problems, or whatever work-related things they would like to discuss

- Play down I, me, my, and instead emphasize you and we in discussions with employees
- Use gender neutral language and discourage the use of sexist language
- Brief all employees on the meaning and manifestations of sexual harassment and the organization's policy on sexual offenses

SECTION 6

TOPIC 28

Communicating Effectively in Stressful Situations

Saying No Graciously to Employees

"One must separate from anything that forces one to repeat no again and again"
—Frederick Nietzche

A. Things to Know

- Managers can't be expected to say yes all the time. It is in the nature of things for them to say no to certain matters such as requests and suggestions.
- Saying no requires that a manager possesses the courage to do what he/she believes to be right. There is no need for a manager to have guilt feelings when saying no when it makes sense to do so.
- Managers can earn more respect by giving a responsible no than giving an irresponsible yes.
- Many managers find the need to say no to their employees to be one of the hardest things they have to do because they are reluctant to run the risk of offending valued employees.
- A decision to say no must be responsible and objective. It should be carefully considered and based on sound reasons. It should never be arbitrary or merely to show employees he/she is the boss.

- It is irresponsible for a manager to say yes to a request or suggestion just to be nice or to avoid the possibility of making the employee unhappy.
- A manager's clear and definite response of no saves time and avoids giving the employee false hope by delaying an answer.
- Managers should not delay an answer to a request when they know that the request has to be denied. A delayed answer wastes time and creates anxiety.
- It is best for managers to say no firmly and leave no doubts that the answer is no by wording, voice tone, and body language.
- It is important for managers to show employees that they have given careful consideration to their requests or suggestions. It is best to take the necessary time to think over an answer when it involves a significant expenditure of time or money.
- When a manager needs time to think about a request or suggestion, he/she can make statements such as these:
  1. "Let me get back to you on this in a couple of days."
  2. "Your idea is worthy of serious consideration so let me refer it to the finance committee for its input."
  3. "Give me a little time to consider the pros and cons of your suggestion and I'll be back to you on it next week."
  4. "This is so important that I want to clear it with my boss before giving you the go ahead on it."
  5. "Your idea appears to have merit, but first let me check our policy to see that it permits this kind of action."
- Say yes to reasonable requests and suggestions. It is imperative that managers avoid being classified as Mr. or Ms. "no no" because of their negative attitudes on most matters.
- There is a way to say no in a way that is polite, kind, and gracious, and that enables the manager to maintain goodwill with the employee whose request was rejected.
- It is essential that managers demonstrate a sincere interest in their employee's ideas and that they deserve serious consideration before a decision is made.

- Managers should explain clearly, in plain language, and in a forthright manner the reasons for denying a request.
- The way managers say no influences how their employees react to a negative answer.
- It is a good idea for managers to see if they can't build on the employee's suggestion to see if it can be made to work rather than rejecting it outright. Managers should have an attitude of "how can we make this work" rather than "the trouble with that suggestion is."

B. Things to Do

- Act confident rather than hesitant or defensive when saying no to suggestions.
- Avoid apologizing or making excuses when denying suggestions.
- Listen intently and show a genuine interest in what the employee is suggesting and don't interrupt except to clarify something.
- Listen patiently and seriously to the entire suggestion before reacting.
- Take time to consider the suggestion carefully rather than listening superficially and merely going through the motions.
- Do your best to understand what the employee is proposing.
- Weigh the pros and cons of the suggestion objectively and consider the consequences before you reject the idea.
- Give the suggestion fair and reasonable consideration before making your decision to deny the suggestion.
- State your answer candidly, concisely, and without sugarcoating it (don't dwell on your no answer; just give it and move on).
- Respond to questionable suggestions clearly and firmly by saying something like this, "I don't think I could justify doing that" or "sorry but that is something I don't do."
- Avoid acting irritated or bothered by certain employee's frequent ill-considered suggestions by making sarcastic or insulting remarks while rejecting their suggestions. For

example, "oh no!—not another suggestion" or "why don't you just do your job?"

- State the problem and negative results that would occur if the suggestion were approved. Better yet, put a few questions to the employee to lead him/her to see why the suggestion wouldn't work.

- Say no to requests face-to-face to the employee in a decisive but courteous manner.

- If the rejection of an employee's suggestion is going to cause ill feelings, and involves other departments, have all the managers who would be affected by the negative decision join you in the rejection.

- Be sure to express your appreciation for thoughtful suggestions and the employee's desire to be helpful when saying no to the suggestion.

- Develop "personal policies" to help you feel less guilty when saying no to employee's suggestions. "Personal policies" are a set of simple rules that guide your decision and actions. "Personal policies" help you to define your priorities, e.g., I don't make spur-of-the-moment decisions on important matters.

- "Personal policies" work because they remove rejection from the situation—you are not saying no to the person's idea or suggestion but merely upholding your own policy.

- Saying "I don't do that" to a request is more successful than "I can't" because it is more convincing and impersonal.

- Invite employees who have previously made worthwhile suggestions that were implemented to continue sharing ideas with you in the future.

Responding to Complaints by Angry Employees

"Self-control means controlling the tongue,
a quick retort can ruin everything"

—Proverbs

A. Things to Know

- Employee problems and complaints are among the most time-consuming aspects of a manager's job.
- Imagined complaints are as important and serious to the complaining person as are complaints that are based on facts.
- Employees with unjustified complaints are entitled to express them as are employees with justifiable complaints.
- Most employees consider their complaints to be real and valid.
- Employees airing complaints are not always seeking solutions but simply airing them because employees want to be listened to and have the chance to ventilate.
- Managers need to be careful not to mistake a complaint about a specific matter for an employee's general dissatisfaction with the job.
- It is better for complaints to be aired openly than for them to be expressed underground.
- Three things are usually on the mind of a person with a complaint:
  1. To tell a manager that something is wrong
  2. To find out what the manager is going to do about it
  3. To learn what the manager is going to do to ensure that the problem isn't repeated.
- There are typically four things on the mind of the manager receiving the complaint:
  1. Something is apparently wrong
  2. Who is at fault?

3. How can the matter be settled fairly and to the satisfaction of both the complaining person and the organization?
4. What needs to be done to prevent the problem from occurring again?

- The way managers treat a complaining employee at the beginning of the interaction can set the tone for the entire discussion and affect how the complaint is resolved.
- Managers are instinctively inclined to respond to an angry employee in either of two ways:
  1. Stand their ground and "fight"
  2. Suppress their feelings, say nothing, and walk away (this is the "flight response"). Obviously, neither of these actions is effective or appropriate.

     Managers confronted by an angry employee with a complaint should remember to use the three Cs approach: (1) be calm, (2) be cool, and (3) be collected. Managers should show instant interest and concern and listen without interrupting until the employee has finished airing his/her complaint. It is a big mistake for managers to try to defend themselves, or the statements or actions causing the anger, while the employee is still angrily expressing his/her complaint.
- Anger is a normal human emotion. It is healthful for an employee who feels mistreated to express his/her resentment.
- The manager's showing of interest and concern along with attentive uninterrupted listening, helps the employee's anger to dissipate.
- A manager can't control an employee's anger, but he/she can control his/her way of reacting to the anger being expressed (don't let the employee press your anger button).
- Managers should concentrate on the nature of the complaint and find a fair solution to it and not be influenced by their attitude toward or feelings about the particular employee.
- Be sure to write up the relevant facts and details regarding the complaint and how it was resolved for the record.

- Remember that in all emotional situations the goal is to generate light rather than heat.

1. Recommended Attitude for Handling Employee Complaints:

- View all complaints as important; don't minimize or downplay any complaints.
- Feel empathy and show concern for the employee's unhappiness.
- Try to view the complaint the same as the employee does in order to understand the reasons for the employee's anger.
- Perceive a complaint as an opportunity to correct a problem and improve something.
- Think objectively about the complaint and refrain from reacting based on the person issuing the complaint.
- Accept the fact that every employee has the right to air complaints in an acceptable manner.
- Keep an open mind concerning the complaint; delay any judgment until you secure all of the facts and consider them.
- Seek to keep on top of things by maintaining an open-door policy and use the technique of managing by wandering around (MBWA).
- Understand that most employees will suffer in silence or gripe to their coworkers—you can't rely on an employee with a complaint coming to you to discuss it.
- Convey the attitude that you are both approachable and accessible to employees.

2. The Three Stages of Dealing with a Complaint

- The three stages are: (1) the opening stage, (2) the fact-finding stage, and (3) the closing stage.
  1. The opening stage:
     - Meet with the employee with the complaint promptly and privately.
     - Try to get the person seated and calmed down.
     - Sit at the same height and eye level. If the employee acts extremely hostile, keep a safe distance away. Refrain from touching the person in any way.

- Show your concern immediately. Avoid acting defensive, confrontational, or resentful.
- Remember that an angry employee is usually not upset with you personally, so don't take the anger being expressed personally; instead act composed and let the person express his/her frustration (act like a sponge).
- Provide adequate time for the discussion and don't act rushed (instruct your office assistant that you don't want to be interrupted).
- Make the employee feel important and that you take his/her complaint seriously.
- Control your own emotions and avoid acting angry or upset. Above all, don't act antagonistic toward the person.
- Listen and don't say anything other than to assure the employee of your genuine concern and desire to find a fair solution to the problem (be sure to make this concern known at the start of the session) the angry employee wants to emote at this time and any comments by you would be either ignored or only further antagonize the person.
- Listen with an open mind and delay any judgments until you have the employee's full story and have gathered all the facts.
- Delay trying to say anything until the employee's anger has ended. You can detect this by observing the changes in the person's voice tone and volume, rate of speaking, and body positioning.
- Acknowledge that you have "got the message" by saying something like this, "Archibald I can see that you are angry and frustrated. I am concerned about this and am here to listen to anything you would like to tell me."
- Show that you understand the complaint by saying something like this, "You are angry because your coworker Bruiser hit you on the head with a brick, that your head hurts, and you want him fired immediately. Do I understand you correctly?"
- Demonstrate your compassion by stating something to this affect, "I know how much it must hurt to get hit by a brick and

we shall take appropriate action as soon as we can consider all of the facts."

- Once you have achieved your twin purposes of getting Archibald calmed down and secured his perception of the situation, it is time to hear Bruiser's account of the incident to determine if there were any extenuating circumstances.

2. The fact-finding stage

- Continue to gather information by questioning Archibald in greater detail. Do this in an interested but nonintimidating manner to clarify what he said, or failed to say. For example, could you tell me more about what was going on when Bruiser threw the brick?
- Limit the time you talk so you can secure more information from the person complaining.
- Take notes unobtrusively on the key points the employee has stated for the record (it is a good idea to explain why you are taking notes so the employee won't feel intimidated).
- Invite questions form Archibald and answer all of these questions candidly and precisely rather than in a wishy-washy or evasive way.
- Complete your questioning to obtain any additional information and explain the next steps in the fact-finding procedure.
- Ask Archibald what he thinks would be a fair solution to the problem and make sure you understand his answer.
- Gather additional facts by questioning Bruiser to get his side of the story.
- Interview any witnesses to the brick throwing or people who know anything pertinent to the incident or events leading up to it.
- Be sure to differentiate between facts, opinions, and inferences expressed by the people questioned.
- Meet again with Archibald and present him with all the facts you have gathered. Ask Archibald to react to the total information available concerning the incident.
- It is essential that you don't disclose the sources of the information in specifics—just that you have talked with anyone who could provide relevant information.

- Ask Archibald to react to the total information available and whether he still had the same recommendation for a solution.
- Discuss the facts with Bruiser and obtain his reactions and what he considers a fair solution.
- Assure both parties to the incident that you will consider all the facts fully and will decide the matter in as fair a manner as possible and as soon as possible.

3. The closing stage
- Schedule a joint meeting with both employees involved in the incident to inform them of your decision and the reasons for it. (Suspension or Termination is an option.)
- Explain the decision-making process without violating anything said in confidence.
- Emphasize that the decision was made after utmost consideration and in an ethical and objective manner.
- Provide both employees with a reasonable opportunity to ask questions about anything relevant to the decision.
- Respond to all appropriate questions confidently, candidly, and without acting defensive or irritated.
- Ask both men if they have anything they would like to say about the decision.
- Study the body language of both men to provide you with feedback on how they really feel about the decision.
- Inform both men in a firm manner what you and the organization expect from both of them in the future and if the friction were to continue that either or both would be dismissed.
- Conclude the meeting on a positive note and with a statement that you wished them well and are confident that they will work cooperatively together in the future (or you may suspend or terminate Bruiser).
  NOTE: Organizations with unions will handle grievances as called for in the union contract.

TOPIC 30

Sharing Bad News Compassionately with Employees

"Though it be honest, it is never good to bring bad news"
—William Shakespeare

A. Things to Know

- There are two kinds of bad news managers may need to share with their employees:
    1. That of a personal nature, for example a serious car accident involving a family member.
    2. That of a professional nature, for example the layoff of the employee.
- We shall deal with the sharing of bad news of a personal nature in this book; however, much of the information applies equally well to job-related bad news.
- Employees are entitled to hear the truth regarding bad news and managers have an ethical obligation to state the bad news to them candidly as soon as they have the essential facts.
- Nobody likes to share bad news with anyone; however, as a manager, you will need to accept the responsibility for sharing bad news of both a personal and job-related nature with your employees.
- There are five factors a manager should remember for sharing bad news with employees:
    1. Share the bad news in a private and comfortable place where no one can see or hear what is happening.
    2. Create a permissive climate which encourages the employee to feel free to ventilate and express his/her feelings fully.

3. Offer support by statements and actions indicating you understand the seriousness of the situation and are empathetic for the person.
4. Get the best person available to offer emotional support and any necessary assistance, for example, employee's best friend at work, family member, or minister.
5. The manager needs to be willing to offer unconditional support to the employee.

- Managers need to be willing to interact with the employee as a fellow human being.
- Managers need to view the matter as an interaction of two people who are doing their best to make it through a difficult and stressful situation.
- The situation calls for the manager to have a heart-to-heart and gut-to-gut interaction rather than a mind-to-mind interaction.
- The manager's role is primarily "to be there" for the employee and to concentrate on the employee's needs and feelings.
- It is imperative that managers not only feel empathy for the employee, but that they also demonstrate their compassion by means of their facial expressions, body positions, words, and voice tone.
- When sharing the bad news it is essential that managers balance the need to be objective regarding the information being delivered and that of having compassion for the employee.
- Managers need to avoid becoming so personally involved with the situation that they lose their ability to view the situation clearly and objectively.
- Managers have no need to feel guilty or apologetic when sharing the bad news. Granted, it is an exceedingly unpleasant responsibility, but it has to be done and done to the best of the manager's ability.
- Managers instinctively want to soften the blow when sharing bad news, but they need to resist this temptation in order to be certain that the severity of the situation is not lost because of the way the news is presented.

- There are two important things for a manager to consider when preparing to convey bad news to an employee:
  1. How to best state the bad news and how to adapt your approach and wording to the employee's personality and the situation.
  2. How to listen and respond most effectively; for example, how to show compassion for the feelings being expressed by the employee.
- A manager can expect and needs to be prepared to deal with a wide variety of reactions from the employee's receiving the bad news such as:
  1. acting exceedingly composed, even though churning internally;
  2. sitting numbly in apparent shock;
  3. denying the reality of the news;
  4. breaking down completely with violent sobbing.
- The method of sharing the bad news depends on the employee's personality, the timing, the urgency of and type of bad news and the closeness of the manager-employee relationship.
- It is important that the best person for the employee share the bad news.
  1. If the bad news is of a personal nature it is desirable that a person who has a close and trusting relationship with the employee share the bad news (however, this assumes that the person is readily available).
  2. If the bad news is related to the employee's work, it is preferable that the bad news be presented to the employee by someone with authority who is respected by the employee.

B. Things to Do

- Managers need to be and act sensitive, sincere, and genuine throughout the interaction.
- Managers should act concerned for and focus all their attention on the employee. Conversely, they should not act embarrassed, apologize, or feel guilty over delivering or bringing the bad news.
- Gather and confirm all the relevant facts regarding the situation before saying anything to the involved employee.

- After learning about the bad news, the manager needs to consider who should be present when he/she delivers the bad news.
- The manager needs to select the best time to share the bad news. This should be delayed until all the essential facts are known unless conveying the news requires immediate notice because of the urgency of the situation.
- Select a quiet and private place to share the bad news.
- .It is best to have a comfortable chair or sofa in the room with a restroom nearby.
- The place should allow the employee to remain undisturbed for as long as the employee needs in order to regain his/her composure (the news should not be given in the manager's office because the employee may feel compelled to leave before he/she is emotionally ready to do so).
- There is no one ideal way to share bad news; however, these procedures are worth considering:
  1. Tell your administrative assistant that you don't want to be disturbed (you need to give the employee your full attention and to avoid rushing the interaction).
  2. Invite the employee to meet with you in an appropriate place. Escort the person to a comfortable chair and sit close to him or her.
  3. Get right to the point without sounding abrupt. State the basic facts calmly, simply, and briefly (state only the essence of the bad news; delay any unnecessary details until later in the interaction).
  4. Speak clearly and distinctly without rushing your statements.
  5. Be candid and objective when presenting the facts. Neither overstate nor understate the situation (try to resist the temptation to sugarcoat the facts).
  6. Repeat the important information if it appears advisable to do so or if asked to by the employee.
  7. After stating the bad news the manager should just observe and listen to the employee for clues as to how to proceed.
- In the event the employee remains silent, after hearing the bad news, but his/her facial expressions and body language

indicate he/she is really hurting inside the manager should
encourage the employee to talk by gently commenting with
a concerned tone of voice and caring look, that you are there
to help in any way you can and you are ready to listen to
anything the employee wants to say (touching the person in
a caring manner is often helpful and appreciated).

- Touching is the most powerful way a manager has of
  showing his/her concern and support for the upset employee.
  However, be careful how long and where you touch the
  person to avoid suspicion and criticism. Because of the nature
  of modern society, managers need to be careful with their
  comments and actions even though they are meant to be
  reassuring to the person.

- Managers need to avoid well-intended, but worthless,
  comments such as these: (1) "everything will be alright so
  you don't need to worry about anything"; (2) "God will
  help you cope with this"; or (3) "adversity makes all of us
  stronger."

- After the employee has calmed down and asks for details, go
  ahead and provide them. Also invite any questions and answer
  them honestly.

- Encourage the employee to state his/her thoughts and feelings
  if he/she would like to. If the employee elects to share them,
  then listen attentively without interrupting or making any
  judgmental statements.

- Listen to the employee's word choices, voice tone, and observe
  the body language in an effort to understand what he/she is
  going through at the time.

- Allow the employee to express his/her innermost feelings,
  anger, and grief while reacting to the bad news—act as a
  sponge by letting the employee ventilate fully without your
  saying or doing anything.

- Mirror back or rephrase what the employee has just said to
  you with a soothing and reassuring voice tone accompanied
  by a caring look to demonstrate that you understand and feel
  compassion for the employee's situation.

- Managers can also show that they understand what the employee is going through emotionally by compatible body positioning and movement.
- Ask the employee if he/she prefers to be alone or have someone with him/her after he/she has calmed down and understands the situation more clearly.
- If the employee names another person to be with him/her to provide comfort, promptly contact that person and explain the situation and that the person grieving would like the person's presence to help him/her cope with the situation.
- While the manager and employee are waiting for the person requested to arrive, the manager should repeat his/her offer to help.
- The offer to help should not be a general offer such as "Let me know if I can help you in anyway"? It is better to be specific by asking a question such as "What can I do to help you?" or "How can I help you?"
- Make your offer to help be and sound sincere rather than merely going through the motions.
- Much as you want to be helpful, it is important not to offer unsolicited advice. You may have some excellent advice to offer but the timing is wrong for stating it.

TOPIC 31

Giving and Receiving Criticism Effectively

"People ask you for criticism, but they only want praise"
—William Somerset Maugham

1. Giving Criticism:

A. Things to Know

- The way you criticize can make the difference between an employee whose performance continues to be unsatisfactory or whose performance improves significantly.
- Make your criticism improvement and future oriented instead of focusing on the past and finding fault.
- Constructive criticism enables employees to do their job better and to reach their potential.
- Keep in mind your employee's feelings. Limit the frequency and severity of your criticism to the ability of the employee to absorb what you are saying rather than your need to unload by expressing everything on your mind at once.
- Managers develop their employees by never failing to criticize them when warranted, but doing it in the right way at the right time and in the right place.
- Sarcasm, ridicule, accusations, moralizing, preaching and scolding, and old-fashioned bawling out the person are all inappropriate and counterproductive when criticizing an employee and create resentment.
- Being criticized helps employees know how they are doing and where they stand; they are entitled to be leveled with.
- When criticizing try to get feedback to enable you to ascertain if the employee understands and accepts what you are saying.

- Be candid, clear, specific, and get directly to the point when criticizing an employee. Don't be so general and euphemistic that your point is lost.
- Four factors influence the effectiveness of a person's reaction to your criticism:
  1. Intent of person doing the criticizing
  2. Way the criticism is given
  3. Content of the criticism
  4. Employee's attitude toward the person criticizing and being criticized in general.
- Some managers believe in using the sandwich approach when criticizing. They like to commend the employee for past accomplishments first. Next, they discuss the behavior or performance causing the criticism and finally they compliment the employee about something.
- The critics of the sandwich method feel that it is ineffective because it sends mixed messages and the actual criticism loses its impact.
- People being criticized need to know that managers doing the criticizing often feel much more strongly about the problem being criticized than the way they are stating it to the employee.

B. Things to Do

- Criticize the deed not the person. Be specific rather than general when describing the subject of the criticism.
- Make your point, but do it in such a manner that it allows the employee to maintain his/her self-respect.
- Demonstrate your desire and willingness to be helpful and emphasize that your comments are meant to be constructive.
- Keep the employee's personality, your relationship, and the issue separate.
- Never compare the performance of one employee with any other employee.
- Give only as much criticism as the employee can handle at one time—don't use overkill.
- Be candid while criticizing, but choose your words carefully and avoid using inflammatory, objectionable, and insulting words.

- Be calm and speak with a low-keyed voice.
- Emphasize getting a remedy instead of dwelling on the problem.
- Make sure the employee understands the criticism and the reasons for it.
- Use "I" statements and take responsibility for everything you say to the employee.
- Make sure the employee understands the problem and what he/she needs to do to overcome it. You can achieve this by doing the following:
  1. Define and explain the problem
  2. State the reasons that it is considered to be a problem
  3. Explain the specific improvement expected
  4. Discuss the various solution options and select the best one
  5. Ask the employee to explain the action that is needed to correct the problem.
- Recommended planning procedure before the discussion:
  1. Get all the facts and get them straight. Make sure your information is accurate, complete, and current and that you understand the entire situation.
  2. Identify any extenuating circumstances pertaining to the problem and share the blame for the problem if it is the fair thing to do.
  3. Consider all the possible consequences that could result from your criticism.
- Ask yourself these questions before criticizing anyone:
  1. What is my specific purpose?
  2. Will the employee's reaction be good or bad?
  3. Could the criticism make things worse?
  4. Is my criticism fair and reasonable?
  5. What exactly do I need to say? (not say?)
  6. How can I best say it?
  7. What is the best time and place to criticize the employee?
  8. How can I enhance the person's receptivity to what I have to say?
  9. How can I minimize the employee's resistance and defensiveness?

- Recommended procedure for sharing the criticism:
  1. Select a good time for both you and the employer to meet. However, it is best to meet as soon as you have all the facts about the situation warranting the criticism.
  2. Pick a quiet and private place to meet.
  3. Inform your office assistant that you don't want to be interrupted.
  4. Greet the employee in a pleasant but businesslike manner; avoid any hint of irritation or animosity.
  5. Explain the purpose of the meeting and how you feel about the problem and how it is creating a problem not only for you but the entire department.
  6. Assure the employee of your concern for him/her and that your criticism is meant to be helpful.
  7. Ask the employee to present his/her perception of the situation and listen attentively without any interruptions until he/she has finished talking.
  8. Give your reaction to the employee's explanation and then hold a discussion.
  9. Create a feeling of dissatisfaction within the employee regarding the problem and the desire to overcome it (the employee needs to feel sufficiently uncomfortable so he/she will want to improve).
  10. Ask questions to guide the employee's thinking about the needed improvement without being too directive.
  11. Make some suggestions when the employee has no ideas about how to remedy the situation. Try to identify together as many options as possible.
  12. Agree on the best solution.
  13. Agree on the expected improvement and a target date for it.
  14. Discuss possible ways to make the improvement.
  15. State clearly the consequences of not meeting the expectations for remedying the problem.
  16. Get a commitment for the corrective action and have the employee sign a paper stating, for the record, what she/he has committed to.

17. Conclude the session with an expression of confidence that the employee has the ability to improve as expected.

2. Receiving Criticism

A. Things to Know:

- Being criticized is a normal and inevitable part of life.
- No one is too wise, too important, too old, or too popular to avoid being criticized by someone, somewhere over something.
- Nobody enjoys being criticized. It is natural to resent getting criticized and to tune it out to protect one's self-esteem.
- A well-adjusted mature person is able to accept constructive criticism and profit from it.
- It is a good idea to proactively ask for feedback regarding your work to show you are open to suggestions on ways to improve your performance.
- If managers never criticized any employee, about anything, no one would ever do anything better.
- Learn to accept constructive criticism in a gracious manner and use it as a catalyst for personal growth.
- The challenge is for the person being criticized to profit from the criticism and to avoid acting resentful or defensive.
- It is essential that the employee being criticized evaluate the credibility of the person making the criticism and his/her motive for the criticism.
- Avoid the mistake of confusing the person offering the criticism with the value and substance of the criticism (even a complete SOB can offer worthwhile criticism).
- Once you understand the criticism, it is crucial to refrain from making excuses or tuning out the critic. Consider whether the criticism is fair. If you believe it to be unfair explain why calmly and without being abrasive.

B. Things to Do

- Demonstrate to people, by words and actions, that you are receptive to their suggestions and criticisms
- Accept and be receptive to the criticism and respond in the spirit in which it was given.
- View the criticism as something about your specific conduct or performance rather than as a criticism of you as a total person.
- Evaluate the source. Ask yourself if he/she has credibility and is qualified to judge your work. Also notice the critic's mood at the time and try to determine the person's reasons for the criticism.
- Regard recurring criticism seriously because it is probably legitimate.
- Hear the critic out and control your emotions—don't act defensive or take personal offense. Conversely, show your appreciation if it is justifiable.
- Listen carefully to the tone of voice, choice of words, and observe the person's body language for clues as to the critic's attitude at the time.
- Listen attentively and ask for additional information if needed.
- You can encourage the critic to furnish you with more specific information by asking questions.
- If conditions warrant it, ask for time to digest the information and request a follow-up meeting to discuss the matter more fully.
- After considering the criticism, if you feel it was unwarranted, share your reactions and the reasons for feeling that the criticism was unjust.
- Here are some positive statements and questions you could make and ask when being criticized:
  1. "Hmm, that is something I never thought of, can you tell me more about that?"
  2. Could you give me some specific examples so that I can understand your point better?

3. "I'm a little unclear about your point, could you clarify it for me?"

4. "Thank you for your willingness to share your viewpoint with me, I appreciate it."

5. "I get your point, what do you think I should do?"

- Jointly summarize the main points discussed regarding the problem, what is expected in the future, and any help that is available.

TOPIC 32

Giving and Receiving Apologies Gracefully

"Oh, words are action enough, if they're the right words"
—D.H. Lawrence

1. Making Apologies

A. Things to Know:

- We are all wrong at times and need to apologize to the people we have wronged.
- Apologies can be a positive thing when offered and received in the right way. They make all concerned feel better.
- Secure people are able to apologize when fairness dictates that it is fair to do so.
- Managers need to realize that apologizing does not weaken their authority or power.
- Employees respect managers who have the courage to apologize when appropriate to do so.
- There are times when a manager is not sure he/she is wrong, but can plainly see that because of a recent interaction relations are strained. Under these conditions, the manager can make a limited apology that does not admit any wrongdoing but opens the door to reconciliation. He could say, "Janice, it seems that you are upset with me and I regret this."
- The manager could also make a limited apology by saying this, "Bill, if I did something to offend you it was unintentional and I regret it if you feel I did something to hurt your feelings, I certainty did not intend to."
- In the final analysis, it isn't who was right or wrong but what is right that counts.

- Big people are willing to apologize. It is the small person who refuses to apologize even when it is warranted.
- People who have been offended feel better when they receive a sincere and prompt apology.
- Apologies help heal damaged relationships and help maintain good relationships.
- Successful apologies have four components:
  1. The person apologizing acknowledges the wrongdoing and accepts responsibility for it.
  2. The person offers an explanation for the offensive behavior.
  3. The person expresses regret.
  4. The person offers reparation.

B. Things to Do

- Be sincere when apologizing—don't just go through the motions.
- Apologize promptly when you realize an apology is needed and deserved.
- Get right to the point without acting rushed and eager to get it over with (don't ramble and hem and haw when apologizing).
- Refrain from acting reluctant, hesitant, or embarrassed when apologizing.
- Apologize to the person in private unless you made the offensive statement or action in front of other people. In this instance, make your apology in front of the same people.
- Apologize graciously with a straightforward simple statement such as, "Gerry, I sincerely regret getting angry with you yesterday and I'm sorry I was so hard on you."
- Refrain from asking for forgiveness.
- Avoid making excuses for what you said or did; keep the focus on making things right with the person you're apologizing to rather than attempting to justify your behavior.
- Maintain steady eye contact while apologizing.
- Apologize face-to-face rather than by telephone or e-mail.

2. Accepting Apologies

A. Things to Know:

- The person receiving an apology can minimize the awkwardness and discomfort of the situation by smiling, being friendly, and extending his/her hand immediately after the apology.
- When accepting heartfelt and sincere apology, you should avoid gloating, making any disparaging comments, and causing the person issuing the apology to feel embarrassed (don't make the person apologizing "eat crow").
- Accept the apology graciously and avoid rebuffing the person offering the apology by saying, "I don't know why you are apologizing, it really isn't necessary" or "I was wondering when you were going to apologize."

B. Things to Do

- Accept the apology graciously in a friendly manner.
- Receive the apology without acting embarrassed.
- Accept the apology willingly and without any hint of reluctance or resentment.
- Maintain eye contact—don't look down or away.
- Consider making these kinds of comments to ease the anxiety associated with this kind of situation:
  1. "I accept and appreciate your apology."
  2. "I accept your apology, but I want you to know that I feel I contributed to the problem and regret doing so."
  3. "Thank you; I recall having goofed on occasion myself"—said with a smile.
- Immediately extend your hand after receiving the apology and shake hands firmly.

TOPIC 33

Communicating Calmly During a Crisis

"The crisis of yesterday is the joke of tomorrow"
—H.G. Wells

A. Things to Know

- Some type of crisis is inevitable for organizations. The type and timing of a crisis is unpredictable. The only safe course is to be adequately prepared in advance.
- Planning for communicating during a crisis is imperative and will determine how effectively the crisis will be handled.
- The crisis communications plan should be an integral part of the organization's overall planning.
- A crisis can be defined as an unstable or crucial time or situation in which a decisive change is pending.
- Common characteristics of a crisis include:
  1. An element of surprise—it is sudden and unexpected
  2. Insufficient information is available during the crisis
  3. Managers feelings of uncertainty and that things are out of control
  4. A sense of urgency exists with little time to think and get organized.

1. Setting Communications Goals for Coping with a Crisis:

- To develop a communications plan when things are normal and before a crisis occurs
- To keep the big picture in mind and avoid getting lost in the details
- To anticipate events that might occur during a crisis and have a plan of action ready to deal with the crisis
- To think calmly and methodically and to avoid making spur-of-the moment decisions or engaging in ill-advised actions or making speculative comments (especially to the news media)

- To assign responsibilities to carefully selected employees and to make these employees known to all members of the organization
- To have management project a confident and reassuring image during the crisis
- To gather accurate information about the crisis as soon as possible
- To control and coordinate all the information collected and disseminated
- To send clear, candid, and consistent messages to appropriate people throughout the crisis
- To show the employees and public that management is on top of things
- To assure employees and the public that order is being restored as quickly and efficiently as possible.

2. Developing the Crisis Communications Plan:

- The first step is to identify and list all potential crises and to develop a comprehensive crisis communications plan for each potential crisis.
- It is important to prepare for the worst possible crisis without unduly alarming the employees.
- The comprehensive communications plan should include the following:
  1. An action plan for each potential crisis
  2. Details for each action plan including specific procedures to be followed for each crisis
  3. Written approval of the plans by top management and the nine member crisis communication advisory council (council duties are explained later in this section)
  4. The responsibilities of people on the crisis communication advisory council should be made known to all employees.

3. Staffing Needed to Handle Crises:

- One of the most important things to do is to identify the different functions needed to cope successfully with a crisis.

Next, people need to be chosen to perform each of these functions.

- Most organizations will need to include these kinds of people to staff the various crisis coping functions:
  1. Representatives from top management to show their support
  2. Security staff to maintain control and order, access to the area as well as any other security matters
  3. Communications advisory council to help design, monitor, and implement the plan. The council should be composed of employees, organization wide, who can work cooperatively together and remain calm under pressure
  4. The communications crisis center should have a director, assistant director, and other interested and competent people to assume all the essential responsibilities and functions of the center
  5. Augmented staff of telephone operators to handle the numerous phone calls concerning the crisis
  6. Representatives from the community such as fire and police departments, medical staff, gas and electric companies
  7. A spokesperson for the organization who represents and speaks for management. He/she has carefully defined duties and authority commensurate with his/her responsibilities.

4. The Qualifications of the Spokesperson:

- The spokesperson should be highly qualified and have the full support of management. He/she should possess these qualifications:
  1. Credibility with the organization's employees, the news media, and community leaders
  2. Trained for and knowledgeable of all of the duties of a spokesperson
  3. Skilled communicator, especially in speaking and writing
  4. Objective thinker with sound judgment and the ability to multitask
  5. Intelligent with the ability to make quick decisions in the midst of turmoil and uncertainty
  6. Healthy with exemplary attendance record and the ability to work long nonstop hours

7. Willing to be on call 24 hours a day and 7 days a week
8. Secure as a person with the ability to deal with confusion, fast changing, and dangerous conditions as well as excited upset people
9. Liked and respected by all kinds of people

5. Authority of the Spokesperson:

- It is essential that the spokesperson have the necessary authority and freedom to fulfill his/her responsibilities (without being interfered with or second-guessed by others in the organization or community).
- The spokesperson needs to have the authority to:
  1. have ready access to top management and the director of the crisis communications center at all times;
  2. speak for the organization with a unified voice;
  3. share appropriate information at the times he chooses;
  4. be limited only by the need to get top management's approval before sharing highly important information.

6. Functions of the Crisis Communications Center Members:

1. Select the location and facility for the center (also the backup location and facility)
2. Provide input into the organization's crisis communications plan along with the input to the crisis communications council
3. Identify the resources needed to implement the crisis plan
4. Distribute copies of the crisis communications plan to all involved employees and others affected by the plan
5. Keep extra copies to give new employees when they begin work
6. Provide indexed loose leafed binders containing the communications plan to allow for easy and continuous updating
7. Prepare a laminated wallet-sized copy of the essential information regarding the crisis plan for all members of the crisis center staff so they will have immediate access to key information at all times
8. Prepare general information packets about the organization ahead of time to be made available to the news media and appropriate community agencies when crises occur

9. Collect and coordinate all crisis-related information
10. Establish clear and definite information clearance and review procedures for disseminating information
11. Conduct simulated crisis exercises to discover the strengths and weaknesses of the current plan (after analyzing the results and making the necessary revisions, it is advisable to hold follow-up simulated exercises).

7. *Information for Spokesperson to Share:*

- The spokesperson should issue a prepared statement as soon as the crisis occurs and before all the details are known that includes:
  1. Stressing that the organization is aware of and is dealing with the situation
  2. Stating that the details are currently being investigated
  3. Pledging to share all appropriate details as soon as they become known and authorized by management
  4. The spokesperson should speak from a prepared statement whenever possible and avoid making comments spur-of-the-moment or in the heat of the moment.
- After the details of the crisis become known, this kind of information should be shared with appropriate individuals and groups:

    Type of crisis; (2) location of crisis; (3) extent of damage or injuries; (4) consequences of crisis; (5) cause if known; (6) time and date of crisis; (7) corrective action being taken.
- The times of briefings should be announced as a convenience to the media (keep in mind media deadlines)
- The spokesperson should avoid:
  1. giving inaccurate information when feeling under pressure;
  2. providing information prematurely or unconfirmed;
  3. making ill-advised statements that damage the organization's reputation;
  4. releasing the names of employees injured or killed before their families are notified;
  5. saying anything that needlessly alarms, upsets, or harms people.

- The spokesperson should offer as much information as possible in an open, frank, and straightforward manner and if necessary provide evidence and substantiation for what he/she is saying.
- The spokesperson's statements need to be as accurate and objective as possible and avoid being either overly optimistic or pessimistic.
- When information is not available, or hasn't been cleared, the reasons need to be stated honestly along with a statement promising to reveal the information as soon as it has been verified and cleared by top management.
- It is a big mistake to answer "no comment" to questions asked by the news media because this creates suspicion and alienates the questioners.
- Any hint of a cover up should be avoided vigorously.
- Briefings should be held regularly and routinely to update the news media and to keep the employees and people in the community informed. Later, after the crisis is over, the spokesperson should issue a final statement including: (1) cause of the problem; (2) how the problem has been corrected and will be avoided in the future; and (3) thanking individuals and groups involved for their cooperation and assistance

8. Distribution of Information about the Crisis Communications Plan:

- The plan should be widely distributed and adequately discussed.
- A condensed version of the plan should be given to all of the employees.
- A detailed version of the plan needs to be distributed to (1) management; (2) supervisors; (3) the spokesperson and assistant spokesperson; (4) security staff; (5) members of the crisis communication center; (6) members of the crisis communications advisory council; (7) the maintenance department.
- Remember to share the information with nighttime employees also.

- A condensed version of the plan should be distributed externally to: (1) fire and police departments; (2) hospitals and medical groups as well as electrical and gas company representatives

9. Crisis Communications Center Functions and Facilities:

1. The facility:
   - Two crisis center locations need to be chosen.
   - The primary site needs to be located in a safe place but close enough to the center of the organization's main activities to keep track of what is happening during the crisis.
   - The main location needs to be on site but the backup location should be nearby off-site
   - The primary site should be fireproof, waterproof, and have shatterproof windows if possible.
   - The main site needs two separate rooms—one for the center's staff to work in and one to store supplies and equipment.
2. The crisis communications center's functions:
   - The center has several important functions
   - Serve as a meeting room for crisis communications advisory committee and center staff
   - Assistant members of the crisis team
   - Provide space to store supplies and equipment
   - Gather all incoming and outgoing information in one central place
   - Prepare information for distribution to various groups
   - Verify facts and make them available to interested parties
   - Serve as contact point for people trying to combat the crisis
   - Maintain a list of key people: phone numbers, pages, e-mail addresses, and home addresses of employees with crisis-related responsibilities
   - Checking in and out of crisis team members and keeping track of their locations
   - Aid the security staff to control access to prohibited areas

10. The Crisis Communications Advisory Council

- Composed of approximately nine members

- Membership should include:
    1. Member from top management
    2. Member of middle management
    3. A supervisor
    4. Director of crisis communications center
    5. Member of security staff
    6. Representative from public relations department
    7. Director of organization's communications department
    8. & (9) Two senior employees.
- The council is responsible for the planning and oversight of the organization's communications activities

TOPIC 34

Disagreeing Diplomatically with your Boss

"A good listener tries to understand thoroughly what the other person is saying. In the end, he may disagree sharply, but before he disagrees he wants to know exactly what it is he is disagreeing with"
—Kenneth A. Wells

A. Things to Know

- Every employer has the right to disagree with his/her boss as long as it is done in an appropriate manner.
- Employees have an ethical obligation to speak up and disagree with any plan, decision, or action that appears to be ill advised or detrimental to the organization and its employees.
- Employees need to be willing to be candid. It is both dishonest and dishonorable for them to agree with something they actually disagree with.
- All employees are responsible for being as open and candid with his/her boss as the relationship or situation permits. No enlightened manager expects a colleague to be a "yes man" or a "nothing person" who never has an idea or opinion of his/her own.
- Managers who convey a dislike for their worker's independence and different ideas inhibit problem solving and dry up creative thinking.
- It is important for employees to know how solid their boss is with his/her boss and how much power and freedom his/her boss actually has to make decisions on his/her own.
- The key to disagreeing with a boss is to size him/her up carefully and accurately know what and how he/she thinks, their pet peeves, hang-ups and communication style preferences.
- Before employees state opposing views to their managers they should also know:

1. What subjects or issues can they and can't they disagree with the boss about?
2. What times can or can't they argue a point?
3. How to disagree without being disagreeable

- Employees realize that their future on-the-job success is largely determined by their boss. Therefore, they are often reluctant to disagree too often or too strongly.
- The goal of employees discussing differences of opinion is to be able to disagree without being disagreeable and to object without being objectionable.
- Employees need to show the strength of their convictions on important matters. However, they need to know when and how to back off (perseverance isn't always a virtue).
- Employees need to know how to express their disagreement without putting their boss on the spot and making him/her look bad.
- The bottom line for managers who sincerely want their associates to think, share ideas, and feel free to disagree must first eliminate their subordinates' fears about being open and disagreeing freely with them.
- Employees should make certain that three conditions exist before expressing strong disagreement with the boss:
  1. What is worth disagreeing strongly about
  2. What to go along with without any comment
  3. Whether there is a reasonable chance that the boss's mind can be changed.
- Realize that the person you are disagreeing with usually thinks he/she is just as right as you do. It is wise to avoid taking a position of "I'm right and you are wrong" (the important thing is not who is right but what is right).
- The inherent differences in status and roles among managers can create barriers and interfere with their communicating effectiveness.
- Expect various kinds and intensities of disagreement. These could include:
  1. People can agree in principle and disagree on details
  2. People can agree on goals and disagree on process
  3. People can agree on goals and disagree on priorities.

- When a disagreement can't be resolved with your boss, refrain from circumventing him/her or gong over his/her head unless the seriousness of the situation demands it.
- When an employee has had a reasonable opportunity to air his/her objections about a boss's decision, the employee has an ethical obligation to fully support the boss's decision or action.

B. Things to Do

1. Dealing with Facts:

- Get all the facts and agree they are relevant to the disagreement.
- It is not necessary for a manager and employees to agree on everything they discuss; however, it is essential to be aware of what has been agreed and disagreed to.
- Agree specifically about and the reasons for disagreeing.
- If the boss sticks to his/her position despite compelling opposing facts, this suggests he/she may have a hidden agenda. In this situation, it is essential that you do your best to get the real issues out into the open so they can be dealt with effectively.
- Listen to your boss' counterarguments and hear the boss out without prejudging his or her reasoning and jumping to conclusions. If you want your boss to hear you out, you must be willing to hear him/her out.

2. Use an Effective Communicating Style:

- Try to disagree with your boss face-to-face and in private
- Speak in a calm, low key, and nonemotional manner
- Use neutral and noninflammatory language
- Listen to understand not to refute when trying to gain agreement
- Tailor your communicating style to match that of your boss. Use words that appeal to your boss. For example, if the boss is a pilot, use pilot's lingo; if he/she is a boating enthusiast, use nautical terms; and if a sport's lover, use sports jargon.
- Get on the same wavelength. If your boss likes people to get right to the point, then get right to the point when talking

to him/her. If the boss likes conclusions being stated first followed by supporting or background information, then make your comments in that order.

3. Timing Factors:

- Make an appointment to ensure it is a good time for your boss and enough time for you to express your disagreement—don't just drop by spur-of-the-moment and expect your boss to greet you with open arms.
- Choose the right time to disagree. Learn the best and worst times to discuss important matters with your boss.
- Test the waters before discussing anything important with your boss. If your boss is in a receptive mood, you can immediately state your position and rationale because you feel safe and that you can be frank and assertive. However, if your boss appears to be preoccupied and has only limited time to talk with you, it is best to delay stating your objections to a later time.
- When talking to a busy boss it is advisable to get right to the point and omit any small talk. Tactfully state what you disagree with and your specific reasons. Avoid a long preamble or your boss may get annoyed and consequently become less receptive to your views.
- Give an early notice to your boss as soon as you have valid reasons to disagree with his/her decision or action. Try to air your objection before your boss has made up his mind on the matter.
- Watch for your boss's body language clues as to how he is reacting to your disagreement—you want to be able to back off before you go too far or it is too late.

4. Strategies for Expressing Your Disagreement:

- Build a reputation for having common sense, sound judgment, and consideration for other people's time.
- Obtain all the necessary facts to make your case and to provide an impressive rationale for your position on the matter.
- Distinguish between major and minor areas of disagreement and tailor your tactics accordingly (battle only over major issues).

- Try to get agreement in principle to get the discussion started in a positive direction.
- Emphasize how your boss's decision can be improved upon rather than what is wrong with it. For example, you could say "I think your decision is fundamentally sound, but wonder if it would be even better if we were to. . . ."
- Spell out the benefits that would result from your proposed addition rather than talking about how to replace the entire idea.
- Present your objections in different ways to help convince your boss of the advantages of your dissenting position. For example, show your support by saying something like this, "Boss, as you know, I agree with your ideas on most things, but on this decision I wonder if you would be willing to reconsider this modification for these reasons."
- Partially agreeing with your boss's idea is a wise approach and will make him/her more receptive to your objection. For example, "Boss, in most situations I think your idea would work fine, but at this particular time with all the uncertainties surrounding this matter, I think we would be better off delaying the decision for a while."
- Demonstrate your strong interest in the boss's proposal by asking penetrating questions about costs, timing, union opposition, and other changes required that might encourage the boss to rethink the idea.
- Rephrasing the idea might help the boss to reevaluate the idea. For example, "What would happen if you were to adjust your plan this way?"

5. Create a Climate Encouraging Constructive Disagreement:

- Stay calm and control your enthusiasm when stating your disagreement.
- Never make your disagreeing personal or take disagreement personally.
- View disagreement as merely a difference of opinion and use the word differences rather than the emotionally charged word disagreement.

- Refrain from arguing or getting even with your boss when you can't get him/her to change thinking to coincide with yours.
- Defend your position without acting defensive or aggressive.
- Also don't introduce any major surprises when disagreeing with your boss.
- Remain noncommittal sometimes rather than stating your disagreement with your boss by saying something such as this, "Hmm, that is an interesting concept; I'd like time to think about it if I may."

6. Help Your Boss Save Face When Disagreeing with Him/Her

- Never show disrespect for your boss's ideas, opinions, and reasons for doing or not doing something.
- Always provide your boss with a honorable out and help him/her to save face and look good (never back your boss into a corner).
- Never confront your boss in a way that embarrasses him/her.
- Build your boss up by being 100% supportive and making him/her look good (never show even a hint of engaging in one-upmanship).
- Act humble and state your appreciation for your boss's willingness to consider your objections.
- Accept your boss's right to change his/her position on matters as he/she chooses.

7. Recommended Reaction When Your Disagreement is Disregarded:

- Avoid getting into any win-lose situations with your boss.
- Emphasize to the boss that you support his final decision and that you will give it your full support.
- Accept your "defeat" graciously and strive not to be bitter or take personal offense at your disagreement being discounted.
- Never criticize your boss's opinions, ideas, decisions, and actions behind his/her back to coworkers or members of the public.
- Remember that your boss is the boss and that he/she has the responsibility for making final decisions on matters—not you.

Persuading Employees Who Oppose Your Ideas

"A man persuaded against his will is of the same opinion still.
A silenced person is not a converted and persuaded person"
—John Murphy

A. Things to Know

- Persuasion is much more than simply asking someone to believe or do something; it is the process of changing people's attitudes, beliefs, and actions.
- To persuade someone you need to speak heart-to-heart as well as mind-to-mind
- In order for your communication to be persuasive, you must:
  1. be understood;
  2. be believed; and
  3. be accepted.
- It is important for managers to constantly bear in mind that people do things for their own reasons not theirs.
- There are two types of persuasive appeals:
  1. to people's reason;
  2. to people's emotions.
- Neither of these types of necessarily more effective than the other. A combination of both types of appeals is usually best.
- People with high intelligence tend to be more influenced than people of less intellectual ability, with persuasive communications based on logical arguments. On the other hand, the high intellectual group will tend to be less influenced by illogical (emotional) appeals or unsupported generalities.
- An employee is most receptive to a manager's ideas when his/her needs and interests are considered.

- You can safely assume that the other person's self-interest will largely determine whether he/she accepts and cooperates with your ideas or rejects them.
- The receivers of your ideas will take action requested if:
  1. the advantage to them is greater than the effort required of them to do something;
  2. the disadvantage to them, as a result of not doing what was requested, is greater than the effort required to do it.
- An additional condition that encourages acceptance of an idea is that it be perceived as feasible.
- You can anticipate opposition to any idea you present by some of the people all of the time, all of the people some of the time, and some of the people some of the time.
- Keep these two admonitions in mind while trying to persuade a person about something:
  1. "A person persuaded against his/her will is of the same opinion still."
  2. "You have not converted a person to your way of thinking because you have silenced him/her."
- A great idea can be introduced at the wrong time and therefore be rejected. Your hope is that the idea will be as Victor Hugo stated it "an idea whose time has come."
- Any person's responsiveness to an attempt to persuade him/her to do something is always influenced by three things
  1. his/her own attitudes, beliefs, and experience;
  2. the nature of the request and existing conditions;
  3. his/her perception of the manager's credibility and motives.
- Be patient when trying to persuade someone. The absorption of ideas isn't easy and takes time. This is especially true when the idea being presented is new and complicated.
- People differ in the time they need to digest new ideas and any attempt to pressure them to quickly agree with any new idea is likely to create resentment or even antagonism.
- The person who is doing the persuading has a significant impact on whether the idea is accepted or rejected. There is more of a positive opinion change if the communicator has high rather than low credibility and is liked and respected.

- The acceptance of your ideas will be significantly enhanced if influential people support them. In fact, support by influential people may have a greater impact on the acceptance of your ideas than the merit of the ideas themselves.
- Mere expression of the communicator's point of view will not, by itself, get the idea accepted—it must be compatible with the feelings and beliefs of the people you are trying to convince.
- Your most persuasive kind of communicating is not what you say, but what you do. If your attitude and actions contradict your words, people will tend to discount what you are telling them.
- Your tone of voice, choice of words, manner of presenting your idea, and your reputation all heavily influence how people react to your ideas and proposals.
- Persuasive communications are most effective when they:
  1. are carefully listened to and understood;
  2. accurately perceived;
  3. considered credible;
  4. relevant and compatible with receiver's needs;
  5. attainable and consistent with receiver's values;
  6. feasible under the existing situation.
- In the final analysis, what really counts when you are attempting to persuade people is not what you tell them but what they believe and accept.
- A number of personal qualities will enhance your credibility and chances of getting your ideas accepted and acted on. These include your: (1) enthusiasm; (2) objectivity; (3) sincerity; (4) expertise; (5) good intentions; (6) trustworthiness; (7) similarity of beliefs and background with the group you are trying to persuade.

B. Things to Do

1. Developing Rapport with Critics of Your Ideas:

- Try to quickly establish rapport and help people to feel relaxed and comfortable around you.

- Show your critics how they will benefit from your proposal and "what is in it for them" at the beginning of your presentation.
- Be sensitive to your critic's needs, desires, and concerns.
- View the ideas you are presenting through your critics eyes and show that you understand and respect their position.
- Give assurances that the idea and its implementation will not jeopardize anyone's job or require any significant change in the way they work (if true).
- Show how your ideas fit into the current ways of doing things and relate to the organization's current goals and present culture.
- Use these compelling words to gain support for your ideas "I need you."
- Find out the critics' "hot buttons" and use them to your advantage.

2. Ways of Providing Convincing Evidence:

- Use an impressive variety of evidence to support your ideas.
- Capture people's attention in order to persuade them to do something. You also need to get people to consider your ideas with an open mind. To do this you need to provide interesting and relevant facts.
- Offer important points to support your ideas at both the beginning and ending of your presentation. Do not put the most powerful points in the middle of your presentation and don't obscure your main points by surrounding them with trivial details.
- Make use of both rational and emotional appeals.
- When using emotional appeals offer logical arguments after an emotional appeal is firmly established. People need to believe that they are being rational when making a decision.
- Where possible, cite the success of your ideas elsewhere.
- Support your ideas with a combination of:
  1. testimonials by credible people;
  2. direct and relevant quotations by authorities on the subject;
  3. impressive statistics;
  4. relevant research findings.

- Include all the facts and figures necessary to convince your critics that your proposal should be accepted.
- Present both sides of an issue when discussing your idea.
- The order of presenting the pros and cons of your ideas strongly influences people listening to your ideas. Giving the proposing information presented first tends to be the most credible and thus more influential than the information that follows. Information offered last also has a strong impact.

3. *Techniques Encouraging Acceptance of Your Ideas:*

- Identify important people who will back your idea.
- If you need to persuade several people of the merits of your idea, make them more comfortable by visiting them, one at a time, in their office.
- Minimize the anxiety over a new idea by showing your critics how the idea builds on existing beliefs and practices of the organization.
- Put forth the most familiar and least objectionable aspects of your idea first to minimize initial resistance.
- Be flexible and willing to graciously accept some changes to your idea so long as the essence of the idea remains the same.
- Introduce only one point at a time to support your idea so your critics won't be overwhelmed and confused.
- Make clear and definite transitions when you leave one point to move onto the next point.
- Show your critics that you understand their view of the matter.
- Be willing and prepared to compromise on some of your ideas but refuse to agree to changes to the basic idea.
- Speak with a pleasant voice tone with a low-key manner and state your points diplomatically. Be certain not to be too aggressive and come across like gangbusters because this will be resented by people opposing your idea (you want to generate light not heat).
- Study your critics' mood fluctuations and adjust your presentation tactics accordingly (get on the same wavelength).

- Know when to remain silent and when to avoid saying more than you need to when stating your idea (you can kill your idea by talking too much).
- Ask questions to help get your ideas across and to get feedback to ascertain if you have been understood.
- Suggest specific actions your critics could take when implementing your idea to minimize their anxiety and to remove uncertainty surrounding the idea.
- Attempt to create a feeling of dissatisfaction with the current situation and a desire to change among the people opposing your idea.

4. Use Persuasive Words:

- To help persuade people use the right words.
- Words by themselves, have a persuasive ability. They can appeal to your critics' emotions.
- Persuasive messages make use of the emotions surrounding certain words. For example, freedom, success, prestige, savings, free, sale, and comfortable bring forth strong emotions that can put critics in a positive frame of mind that will help them accept your idea.
- Choose your words carefully when describing your idea. Avoid negative words such as "this proposal will require major changes" or "this idea will need you to revise your current way of thinking about working overtime."
- State things in a way that doesn't sound like manipulation or high-pressure sales pitches.
- Replace negative and tentative statements with positive and definite statements.
- Use the word when instead of if while making a proposal. For example, "when we make the plan operational it will save us tons of money."
- Make sure your persuasive message includes the eight Cs of an effective communication: (1) current, (2) correct, (3) clear, (4) concise, (5) complete, (6) consistent, (7) candid, and (8) credible.

- Read your persuasive statements aloud to yourself to determine how they sound. Next, ask a couple of coworkers to listen to your statements to provide you with their honest reactions.
- Your goal is to make your points crystal clear yet so tactfully that you don't offend your critics.

5. Dealing with Your Critics' Objections:

- You can expect, regardless of how good your ideas are, that some resistance and rejection will occur. Opposition to your ideas doesn't necessarily mean that anything is wrong with them. Conversely, people sometimes oppose ideas simply because of their nature and because they are negative thinkers.
- It is imperative that you discover what aspects of your idea are seen as pluses and minuses by the people opposing your ideas so you can adjust your persuasive approach.
- Whenever you are trying to convince people of the merits of your ideas, and you are able to predict their objections, address these immediately. This will let the person know that you are aware of and have considered their viewpoints.
- Be realistic; you can't anticipate all objections to your ideas. However, you can predict most objections and be prepared to deal with them.
- When you are stating a point, and don't want to be interrupted, but critics keep interrupting you, you can say something such as "excuse me, I need to make this key point and I would appreciate it if you would let me finish it." You could also say something like this, "Please wait a minute until I finish—I listened to your viewpoints and now I would like you to listen to mine, okay?"
- Reverse positions with your critics by asking them to sum up the reasons you have offered them to support your ideas.
- Remember your goal is to provide a solid defense of your proposal and not to create defiance.

TOPIC 36

Communication Required to Implement Change

"There is nothing more difficult to take in hand, more perilous to conduct, or more uncertain in its success than to take the lead in the introduction of a new order of things"
—Niccolò Machiavelli

A. Things to Know

1. Success in any organization requires continuous change and change management is a major responsibility for all managers.
   - The greatest challenge for managers implementing changes is to introduce the changes in a way that promotes employee understanding, cooperation, and acceptance.
   - The manager's goal is to minimize resistance to, and rejection of, the change. It is to avoid conflict resulting from the adoption of new ideas and practices.
   - Managers prepare employees for changes by continuously promoting a "Let's try it" ethos organization wide.
   - The most effective way to communicate about change builds upon the current beliefs and practices and shows employees what they have to gain from accepting and then cooperating with the change.
   - Employee commitment to a change is most likely to occur when the change is implemented gradually rather than quickly.
   - It is best to have employees participate in the change process from start to finish.
   - Employees will cooperate and accept a change when they perceive that the advantage from the change is greater than the effort to resist it.
   - Peer group consensus is the major influence on an employee's willingness to change.

- New patterns of employee behavior related to a change must be reinforced and rewarded for the change to be implemented smoothly.
- The timing of instituting a change is crucial to its success—it shouldn't be either too fast or too slow.
- The greatest employee receptivity to a change introduced by a manager will be when he/she is viewed by employees as (1) credible, (2) trusted, (3) likeable, and (4) respected.
- Managers should never take resistance or opposition to a change they are making as a personal affront to them.
- If a change is not needed, do not make it.

2. It is important for a manager to have realistic expectations when introducing change. Here are some of the most common ones to expect:
   - The change could make matters worse instead of better
   - Resistance ranges from minor to major
   - Successful implementation of the change may take longer than anticipated
   - Unanticipated problems may occur
   - It may be necessary to modify the nature of the change or build more support to implement it effectively
   - The change may need to be introduced gradually in stages or even delayed until a more appropriate time
   - Rapid and drastic change may cause strong resistance and actually lead to failure of the change
   - It takes time to build support for new ideas and changes
   - Different individuals and groups of employees will react differently to the same change
   - Managers will need to set the pace by being enthusiastic about the change and demonstrating their own commitment to it
   - Managers will need to understand the importance of the employee's feelings and concerns in regard to the change and respond to them in an empathetic manner
   - Managers will need to be readily available to listen in a patient and interested manner to the concerns of the employees
   - Managers will need to give employees plenty of encouragement and opportunities for input and feedback during the transition period

- Managers will need to express their appreciation to the employees for their cooperation and commend them for a job well done after the change has been successfully completed
- Managers should be aware that employees will develop fear and anxiety regarding the change for various lengths of time
- Before making a change managers need the full support of their boss and understand that the change will go more smoothly if there is active support from senior and influential employees.

3. Recommended attitudes of managers who must be willing to:
   - commit to and champion unpopular change;
   - explain things repeatedly to employees and to listen to the same objections again and again;
   - put up with resistance and criticism;
   - deal with conflict;
   - be patient and tolerant;
   - be flexible enough to meet the demands of tense and uncertain situations;
   - adjust to the needs of all kinds of employees;
   - take the time to size up people and situations before saying or doing anything important or controversial;
   - deal tactfully and calmly with any angry and upset employee;
   - take a firm stand against strong opposition;
   - give and receive criticism;
   - be empathetic toward an employee's concerns and fears.

4. The greatest concerns (questions) about change typically expressed by employees include:
   - When is the effective date of the change?
   - How will my job be affected by the change?
   - Will it increase or decrease my freedom to do my job or the control I have over my future?
   - Will I have to work harder?
   - Will I have to receive special training?
   - What are the specific goals of the change?
   - What problems will the change cause?
   - How is the change an improvement?
   - What are the specific reasons for the change?

- What assistance will be available to help implement the change?
- What happens if the change fails or I fail to adjust to the change?
- Will I have a role in the planning or implementation of the change?
- Note: Managers need to deal directly and candidly with these questions to bolster the employee's confidence and to minimize their speculation and fears of the unknown.

B. Things to Do

1. Strategies for gaining support:
   - Pave the way for acceptance by developing the right climate by your daily interacting and communicating with your employees.
   - Minimize the differences and adjustments required by the change and keep as many of the employee's old habits and routines in place as practical.
   - Stress the advantages of the change and cite specifically how the individual will benefit.
   - Point out how uncomfortable and dissatisfied the employees are with the present situation and note the loss of rewards if they continue with the present practices.
   - Offer incentives to employees for accepting the change and successfully implementing it especially if the change is drastic and requires major adjustments by the employees.
   - In the early stages of the implementation obtain the active and enthusiastic support of the following: (1) top management; (2) influential managers and supervisors who are popular and respected by the employees; (3) peer leaders, opinion molders, and key communicators; (4) skeptics or known opponents to the change so they can hopefully become converts and support the proposed changes; (5) avoid including people who dislike each other and have a history of arguing in group discussions
   - Prepare the employees for the change ahead of time by planting the seeds for the change over a period of time rather than springing the change on them suddenly without due notice.

- Introduce a big change gradually by breaking it into small steps to make the change more acceptable and less frightening.
- Ask the employees in the different departments to be affected by the change, to assess how the change will impact them but try to avoid the pitfalls and problems raised by these same people.
- Explain only the essence of the change initially in order not to overwhelm the employees with too much information. After giving employees a chance to digest this information, supply the necessary details and background to enable the employees to fully understand the scope of the changes.
- Discuss the change with employees in small group meetings rather than individually or in large groups.
- Use face-to-face communication about the change to permit immediate employee feedback, a greater sense of participation, and an opportunity for the employees to ask questions.
- .Give employees affected by the change a sense that they can exercise some control over the impact of the change on their work.

2. How to share important information:
   - Share information to the fullest extent possible as soon as the information is available.
   - Releasing information about the general purpose of a planned change, including a general comment about its nature, is preferable to withholding all the information until all the details are known.
   - Share the appropriate amount of information with employees when announcing a change and follow this up with periodic updates regarding the change (this will minimize employees' use of the "grapevine" and the spread of erroneous information).
   - Any single communication pertaining to a change ordinarily is ineffective and minimally changes the viewpoint of most employees.
   - Furnish employees with facts, statistics, expert opinions, and statements by top management supporting the planned change.
   - Cite instances of success with a comparable change in similar organizations to inspire confidence in employees and minimize their fear of the change.
   - Point out the problems with the change but show how other organizations have overcome them.

- Offer your strongest evidence supporting the change first when discussing the change with employees.
- Information about an upcoming change can be communicated in several ways but face-to-face methods are the most effective.
- Effective communicating methods available include: small group meetings; briefings by immediate supervisor; one topic e-mails; business letter addressed to each employee; in-house telephone voice mails; or posting on bulletin boards.
- Explain to employees exactly what is expected of them due to the change.
- Provide reasons for the change that are impressive, convincing, and make sense to the employees affected by the change.
- State what the change is, why it is needed, and how and when it will go into effect.

3. Manager's words concerning an upcoming change can make the difference between the success or failure of a change. Selecting the best words to use is of paramount importance.
   - Know what you want to say and how you want to say it.
   - Choose words and language that are unambiguous and that will be most favorably received by employees.
   - Realize that even a slight difference in words can make a tremendous difference in their interpretation. (Mark Twain once said, "The difference between the almost right word and the right word is the difference between the lightning bug and the lightning.")
   - Use words that are both concrete and specific. Avoid using abstract and general words.
   - Use plain and simple language when explaining a change to help create understanding and acceptance.
   - Ask yourself this question when deciding to use or not use a certain word, "Does the word fill a real need?" If it does, use it, if it doesn't, don't use it.
   - Employ verbal methods to communicate about a change rather than written methods. Your words will be understood better and will lead to prompt feedback.
   - Use words familiar to your employees and that create a mental image for them.

- Seek feedback to determine if you understand what an employee has said to you by asking, "Is this what you mean?" or "Is this what you are saying?"
- Verify that what you have said to an employee is understood by stating, "In your own words please tell me the essence of what I've just said," or ask, "What problems do you see with the idea I've just explained?" Don't let early misunderstandings derail the planned change.

Warning Employees about Tardiness and Absenteeism

"Well begun is half done"

—Unknown

A. Things to Know

- Absenteeism is a term applied to workers failing to come to work for the time they are scheduled to be at work.
- Tardiness is a type of absenteeism that includes (1) coming to work late at the start of the day; and (2) returning from lunch or breaks late.
- Absenteeism and tardiness both create problems for managers and the organization, especially in situations where the employee's work is interdependent and requires coordination.
- The problems of absenteeism and tardiness have two dimensions: (1) frequency and (2) duration.
- Employee absenteeism is considered to be one of the most serious disciplinary problems facing managers irrespective of the type of organization.
- The problems of absenteeism and tardiness are so serious that both offenses can be subject to severe disciplinary action including termination.
- Unfortunately, no simple guide exists for dealing with these problems because the causes are so complex and different.
- Absenteeism is most common on Mondays and Fridays and the workdays immediately before and after holidays. It is also more frequent the day after payday and the first days of activities such as the opening of hunting, fishing, and baseball seasons.
- Absenteeism is caused by both on-the-job factors and off-the-job factors.

- The major causes of absenteeism and tardiness are:
  (1) employee sickness; (2) sickness of a family member;
  (3) accidents at home; (4) transportation difficulties;
  (5) alcoholism and drug addiction.
- It is important to keep accurate and detailed records for
  both absenteeism and tardiness for: (1) individual employees
  and (2) the employees in each department (work unit) for
  documentation purposes.
- Keep track of absenteeism rates. An absenteeism rate is the
  ratio of days lost from work compared to the total number of
  days in which work was available.
- Absenteeism rates are believed to be closely related to
  employee dissatisfaction with (1) the job itself; (2) the
  management; (3) the employee's immediate supervisor; and/
  or (4) with their coworkers.
- When an employee must be absent it is important that he/
  she inform the manager so adjustments can be made in work
  assignments and so the absence can be recorded.
- The employee handbook and the new employee orientation should
  list the only acceptable reasons for both absenteeism and tardiness.
- The employee handbook should present specific and clear
  information regarding what constitutes absenteeism and
  tardiness. It especially needs to define family bereavement and
  the proper use of sick days.
- The most important information covered in the handbook
  should be discussed during the orientation proceedings
  and all employees required to sign that they have read the
  handbook and understand the information it contains (for
  documentation purposes).
- It is crucial that all employees understand attendance
  expectations and requirements and the penalties for
  unauthorized absence and lateness.
- Special care needs to be taken to ensure that employees with
  different cultural backgrounds, or who have limited ability
  to communicate in English and understand important
  information in the handbook.

- Be aware of and follow: the state and federal laws and regulations; the union contract; and the organization's policies concerning absenteeism and tardiness.
- Be aware that absenteeism actions can't unfairly discriminate or adversely impact against any group of employees protected by fair employment laws.
- Be aware that:
    1. the rules must apply equally to all employees regardless of race, religion, national origin, sex, age, or disability;
    2. the rules must be enforced impartially and objectively;
    3. the records should contain the information necessary to prove equal application and enforcement of the work rules.

B. Things to Do

- As a manager it is very important that you know the contents of the organization's handbook well before dealing with a violation of the rules re: absenteeism and tardiness—be sure to review all requirements dealing with these subjects.
- Verify that the employees have received and read the policies and procedures re: absenteeism and tardiness and signed a statement attesting to this fact.
- Be alert to any violations of the absenteeism and tardiness requirements and move quickly to deal with the situation.
- Collect and analyze all of the facts related to the violation so you will be fully informed about the situation when you confer with the employee.
- Contact the offending individual to meet with you privately to discuss the violation.
- State the reason for the session immediately and the problems the person's absenteeism is causing you, the work unit, and the organization.
- Ask the employee to present his/her views of the situation.
- Establish the facts related to the violation as opposed to mere opinions and feelings.
- Discuss the causes of the problem.

- Consider any extenuating circumstances related to the violation and take these into account when making your decision.
- Decide on the actions that are needed to correct the problem.
- Make sure you enforce the rules and point out the consequences if the absenteeism or tardiness were to be repeated.
- Explain that if the problem isn't corrected the employee may need to be terminated.
- Offer to help the employee remedy the problem as needed and appropriate.
- Write up a summary of the decision made and the action taken for the record.
- Place a copy of the report in the employee's personnel file.
- Check to see how things are progressing with the employee in the days following the meeting.
- Note: If the situation warrants discharging the employee, it would be wise to first confer with a human resources specialist, and/or the organization's legal counsel before taking action, especially if the employee being terminated is a member of the protected class.

TOPIC 38

Disciplining Employees Fairly

"It is one thing to show a man that he is in error, and another thing to put him in possession of the truth"

—John Locke

A. Things to Know

1. Please note we are limiting our discussion to the communicating aspect related to disciplining employees. Also, we acknowledge that there are several ways to conduct disciplinary meetings but the process we present is commonly used by managers in all kinds of organizations.

   - The purpose of any disciplinary action is to secure a change in attitude and behavior or to achieve an integration of interests. It is not to degrade, demoralize, nor punish.
   - In most organizations managers view discipline as punishment. However, the word discipline is derived from the Latin word meaning teaching and learning.
   - The disciplinary climate should be serious and business like, yet be conducted with a two-way exchange of thoughts and feelings.
   - Disciplinary sessions are inherently an unpleasant situation for both the manager and the subordinate but they are required if managers and the organization are to operate effectively.
   - Managers who fail to discipline employees when it is needed are not carrying out an essential managerial responsibility.
   - Put disciplinary action in perspective-you are disciplining employees for a specific transgression.
   - It is advisable to limit the amount of information being shared to the capacity of the receiver to accept and understand it, rather than the amount of information you would like to present at the time.

- When discussing a wrongful act, separate the deed or action from the employee as a person.
- Keep control of the session and be professional and poised, but don't be afraid to allow the other person to vent his/her anger without becoming angry yourself. Even though anger begets anger, the fact that someone has blasted you in anger doesn't have to trigger your angry response. Your anger will only produce a similar reaction from the other person and this will lessen the possibility of agreement.
- A disciplinary situation requires leveling. So be frank and forthright. Say it as it is without watering it down.
- The employee should be encouraged to discuss each of the specific problems raised by management. The session will lose much of its value if the manager does all the talking. The meeting is serious but should not be an ugly confrontation. By encouraging input from the employee and setting a positive, tone for the session, the manager will be perceived as a benevolent superior rather than a "bloodthirsty" prosecutor.
- If the employee has been given specific instructions as to what he/she must or must not do in the future, this should be reviewed in detail periodically with him or her. If this is to be a matter which will be included in his/her personnel record, he/she should be made aware of this and to understand how it may affect the employee's future in the organization.
- At the completion of the session, the employee should know exactly where he/she stands and also understand the action you intend to take as a result of the discipline interview and the possible alternatives available. The employee should know that your decision is final. If he/she has recourse through an appeal procedure, he/she should be told the details of that procedure.

2. Recommended attitude for managers when disciplining employees:
   - Focus specifically on the wrongful and expected behavior rather than on the total person
   - Emphasize improvement not punishment
   - Desire to be helpful not punitive

- Be objective toward the problem and compassionate toward the person
- Be determined to maintain your composure and self-control rather than be emotional and "losing your cool"
- Strive to be impersonal and emotionally detached from the situation
- Reject the idea that you can generate good performance by punishing unacceptable behavior
- Expect the need to be flexible while discussing the problem because every employee is different and needs to be treated differently
- Be tough minded without being tough hearted while disciplining someone
- Attempt to avoid holding a grudge toward the person after the disciplinary session.

3. Helping employees keep their self-esteem:
   - Every employee has the right to be treated as an individual with dignity and worth
   - Every employee wants and expects to be respected
   - Employees tend to reject messages that threaten their self-esteem and resent people finding fault with them
   - Severe punishment can damage and sometimes even destroy an employee's self-esteem and self-respect
   - Managers who are skilled at enhancing an employee's self-respect when interacting with them are more likely to be effective when disciplining employees
   - It is a huge mistake to discipline anyone to make an example of him/her or to arbitrarily use mass punishment to discipline a group.

4. Preparing for disciplinary session:
   - The three major objectives of the disciplinary session are: (1) to give the employee notice that his/her work or conduct is unsatisfactory; (2) to counsel the employee on expected performance standards of job conduct; and (3) to offer help and assistance in meeting such standards.

- First be sure of the facts that indicate the person deserves to be disciplined (there is nothing more unfair or demoralizing to a worker than to be falsely accused of something).
- Consider alternative ways of correcting the situation and achieving the desired change or improvement.
- Before saying anything to the employee whose attitude/conduct deserves to be addressed, be sure to do the following to protect the organization and yourself legally:
  1. Review the organization's policies and union contact pertaining to disciplinary actions to make certain the employee's right to due process is being observed.
  2. Be especially careful to protect the rights of people in the protected classes covered by the law and other regulations (e.g., women, racial minorities, the elderly, and disabled).
  3. Routinely discuss your intentions with the Human Resources Department and the organization's Legal Counsel to make sure you are doing the right thing.
- Schedule the session well in advance so you will have adequate time to prepare (e.g., examine personnel record, verify employee's misconduct with other informed people).
- Write down the specific points you need to discuss and how you want to discuss them.
- Make sure the type and amount of information you plan to discuss will be understandable and won't overwhelm the person.
- Schedule a private room to protect the confidentiality of the discussion and prevent public embarrassment.

5. Proper timing of the session:
- Prompt action needs to be taken for serious violations. Corrective action needs to occur as close to the time of the offense as possible.
- When not facing an urgent situation and immediate need for disciplining, try to select a time for the session when: (1) your relationship with the person is reasonably good; (2) you are in a good mood; (3) you believe the person is in a good mood and free of undue pressure; (4) when you are not rushed. Avoid a time when: (1) the person has made a glaring mistake;

(2) the person has recently had an argument with your or another supervisor. Hold the session when: (1) you will not be interrupted by the telephone or e-mail; (2) no one will interrupt your private meeting; and (3) you can both be relatively comfortable and relaxed.

- When you must discipline someone, do it late in the day so the person can have time to adjust before the next day. Although it's tempting to get the action out of the way early in the day, it frequently decreases the person's productivity for the rest of the day.
- If the problem isn't urgent or dangerous but cannot be allowed to continue, it is wise to consider coaching or counseling the person about correcting the problem before disciplining him/her.
- Common sense and fairness dictate that every new employee should have the work rules explained with a give and take "Q &A" period before starting work.
- Change in work rules and procedures need to be shared before they take effect.

A. Things to Do

1. Conducting the disciplinary session:
   - Managers should greet the employee to be disciplined in a business-like manner without acting antagonistic (if manager feels angry or upset at the time it is best to delay the session until he/she has calmed down and can be objective regarding the employee and the situation).
   - Refrain from smiling or you will send a mixed message of both approval and disapproval at the same time.
   - Maintain control and maintain the supervisor-subordinate relationship throughout the session.
   - Conduct the proceedings in an objective, impersonal, and detached manner.
   - Deal with the employee as a unique individual with dignity and do so on an adult-to-adult basis.
   - Immediately inform the employee of the purpose of and reasons for the disciplinary session.

- Be specific by telling the employee exactly what he/she did wrong (e.g., rule violation). Clearly state the effects on his/her offense on the organization and fellow workers, as well as his/her future with the organization.
- Avoid saying or doing anything that can cause misunderstanding regarding the nature of or seriousness of the offense.
- Solicit feedback to ensure the employee understands the wrongful act and the trouble it has caused.
- Describe what the employee has done wrong rather than judging whether it is good or bad, right or wrong.
- Give the employee a full opportunity to state his/her perception of the situation and to offer any related extenuating circumstances.
- The manager listens carefully and hears the employee out, accepts the valid reasons offered, but doesn't accept excuses.
- Get and give feedback. Restate what the employee has said to you to show you understand and have the employee restate in his/her own words what you've said to demonstrate that he/she understands what you said.
- Be constructive and helpful with your remarks. Avoid using a condescending or scolding tone of voice and any abusive or insulting language.
- Answer all employee's relevant questions to the best of your ability.
- Jot down the employee's responses to your probing questions to jog your memory and to have a written record of the session.
- Identify the specific changes the employee needs to make to correct the situation and your expectations regarding the improvement required.
- Point out the consequences if the employee fails to make the necessary improvement and to meet those expectations.
- Discuss the possible solutions to the problem and agree on the best solution.
- Have the employee repeat the nature of the offense, the problems it is causing, and the solution agreed to.

- Impose an appropriate disciplinary action based on the facts of the case.
- Cite the assistance available to help the employee improve.
- Explain the appeals process if one exists in your organization.
- Conclude the session by escorting the employee to the door, shake hands, and express your confidence in the employee's ability to overcome the problem.
- Within a short time after the session, write a summary of the important points covered during the discussion.
- Stop by the employee's workplace 2 or 3 days after the disciplinary session to say "hello" with a smile and a friendly manner. Engage in brief small talk to show you are not harboring any ill feelings toward the person.

Terminating Employees the Right Way

"It is better to be fired for doing the right things than to keep your job while doing the wrong things"

—Unknown

A. Things to Know

- There is no denying that holding a termination session is an extremely distasteful and disagreeable task. However, it is inevitable and an essential part of the manager's job. It is never easy to fire an employee.
- Ruthless as it may sound, the achieving of organizational goals by having effective personnel must be paramount in all personnel decisions.
- The termination session is both a highly objective legalistic matter as well as an emotion charged event. The manager faces the double problem of meeting legal and organizational requirements while also doing what is least harmful to the employee being terminated.

1. Precautions to Observe:

- Make sure during the employee interview and orientation that no manager says anything that suggests that the employment is permanent. Also, nothing written in the employee handbook should state or imply that the employment is permanent.
- Play it safe by consulting with the organization's legal counsel and coordinate all hiring with the Human Resources Department, especially when employing people who belong to the protected group. Also, it is wise to get the approval of your immediate boss and keep him/her fully informed.

- Be certain that you observe both the provisions set forth in the union contract and the organization's policies and procedures when both hiring and firing employees.
- In addition, follow federal and state legal requirements for the employing and discharging of employees. And don't overlook any court decisions that apply to personnel decisions. Pay special attention to all requirements when discharging people belonging to the protected class, which includes racial minorities, women, the disabled, and elderly because they require special treatment.
- Remember the effect that termination has on current employees and any likely negative reactions that the discharge may have on the person's coworkers.
- Be ready to deal with any defensive and emotional behavior by the terminated employee. If you anticipate there may be a highly emotional or aggressive reaction, check to see that a member of the security staff will be close while you are informing the employee of his/her termination.
- It is a good idea to have another manager present as a witness in the event that something occurred during the termination discussion that needs to be verified.

2. Recommended Manager's Attitude While Holding the Termination Discussion:

- After making certain that the legal requirements and organization's needs are met, give the employee's needs a high priority because of the strong emotions involved in termination decisions.
- Show empathy without having any guilt feelings over the need to discharge people for cause.
- Never apologize for needing to terminate a person for cause (justifiable reasons).
- Express yourself in a tactful manner, but be sure you are clear and straightforward so that the employee will understand that he/she has definitely been terminated.
- Remember that the discharged person's self-esteem has suffered a big blow so when leveling with him/her try to provide for the person's emotional needs.

- It is important to treat the terminated employee humanely and ethically.
- Ethical treatment includes:
  1. To have not only the conference but also the entire procedure handled diplomatically, discretely, and compassionately
  2. To be treated as a person with dignity, value, and feelings
  3. To be leveled with regarding the main reason for being terminated (this can be done with candor without undue fear of legal repercussions, as long as the discharge is fair and supported by carefully documented reasons)
  4. To be given an opportunity to react to the discharge and to ask appropriate questions (no arguing should be allowed)
  5. To receive a complete explanation of the kinds of assistance and benefits available to discharged employees.

B. Things to Do

3. Planning the Termination Session:

- There are two main matters managers need to be concerned about: (1) the organization's well-being; and (2) the employees' well-being as a result of the termination.
- Review the entire termination proceedings to meet the needs of both the organization and the discharged employee.
- Check to see that you have met not only all the legal requirements but also the ethical standards of just treatment and common decency.
- It is a good idea to plan the exact wording of your opening and closing statements ahead of time.
- For potentially "explosive" termination situations, it is an excellent idea for the manager who is going to share the "glad tidings" to hold a strategy session with the legal counsel and the human resource affirmative action specialist to receive their advice and suggestions.
- At the strategy session, go over the precautions checklist put together by the human resources specialist and legal counsel and discuss subjects such as:

1. adequacy of the documentation for the action;
2. reasons to state for the termination action;
3. how to word the reasons for the action;
4. key things to say and avoid saying;
5. how to best cope with predicted problems and strong emotional reactions by employee;
6. predict tough questions by employee and how to best answer them;
7. best time and place to hold the termination session;
8. how the termination proceedings are to be recorded and by whom;
9. people to inform, if any, before the termination session and how to do it appropriately;
10. people to inform immediately following the termination action and how to do it;
11. how to develop support for and minimize coworker opposition to the termination, especially if the person was a popular colleague or longtime employee;
12. determining the contents of the severance package and who is the best person to explain it and when to do it.

4. Selecting the Best Time for Termination Session:

- Select the best time for the organization but also consider an appropriate time for the discharged employee.
- Decide on the right amount of time to devote to the session. You don't want to either rush it or prolong it. Avoid getting involved in a long drawn out discussion or defense of the action taken.
- Be sure to reserve sufficient time to provide the necessary information and to answer appropriate questions.
- These important factors should be considered when allocating time to the termination session:
  1. Your relationship with the employee
  2. Employee's position and length of service to the organization
  3. Reasons to be cited for the action
  4. Anticipated reactions by the employee
  5. Usually a termination session should be brief and require between 15 and 20 minutes (without stating details of the severance package).

- There are times that common sense and compassion dictate that you should avoid when terminating an employee. These times include: (1) the employee's birthday; (2) person's anniversary; (3) major holiday; (4) vacation time; (5) recent death to immediate family, impeding surgery, for employee or member of immediate family (you don't want to appear ruthless or heartless to the other employees).
- Opinions vary on the best days of the week to fire someone. It depends on the person and situation.
- The time of the day to hold the termination session is something that should be carefully considered. Late in the day is generally thought to be the best time because it helps save the employee embarrassment and interferes minimally with the coworker's productivity.
- The final step in the termination session is to inform the employee of the precise time and procedure for leaving his/ her workstation and the site. Managers frequently prefer to have the terminated employee leave the premises immediately to avoid having them interact at length with their coworkers (you may find it advisable to play this by ear depending on the person and the situation).

5. Choosing the Place for the Termination Session:

- Never hold a termination session in your office. It is preferable to have the termination meeting in a neutral area, such as a conference room, the employee's office, or a private location in a remote area. It is best to hold it in an area that permits you to leave immediately following the end of the terminating action. If you were to hold the session in your office, it would be harder for you to depart from the meeting site immediately.
- Select a place where the person will not feel compelled to leave right away regardless of his/her emotional state.
- Be compassionate and hold the meeting in a private low traffic area away from other employees.

6. *Conducting the Termination Session*

- Deliver the termination news in person. Tell the employee the news face-to-face. Avoid doing it by phone, e-mail, office memo, inserting in a pay envelope, or by a personal letter.
- Have a witness present when it appears advisable to do so.
- Greet the employee at the door in a businesslike manner without smiling or any small talk.
- Escort the employee to a seat opposite yours with the witness seated to the side.
- Get directly to the point as soon as the employee is settled in his/her seat.
- Look the employee straight in the face when notifying him/her of the termination decision.
- Explain that the action was carefully considered and endorsed by all appropriate people.
- Emphasize that the action is final, irreversible, and when it becomes effective.
- State things tactfully, but not so gently and indirectly that the employee misses the real message.
- Explain briefly, specifically, and honestly the reasons for the discharge.
- Refrain from any insulting or demeaning statements or personal attacks while explaining the grounds for the action.
- Avoid making any trite or self-serving statements such as "Bert, this action really hurts me and I hate to do it and apologize for doing this to you."
- Don't discuss the justification for the decision, defend the action or allow any arguing; however, be willing to answer a few relevant questions.
- Keep calm and composed—don't act at all antagonistic. Allow the terminated person to be emotional—even belligerent—for a short time. It is best to just listen rather than trying to soothe the person while he/she is venting.
- If the person is calm enough to listen and understand information about the severance package that he/she is

entitled to, go ahead and discuss the eligibility, but let the human resources representative explain the details at a later and more appropriate time.

- Inform the employee that everything discussed during the termination session will be kept confidential.

- End the session smoothly and decisively. Don't allow any final comments after you have closed the session—avoid the "just one more thing" comment or series of comments.

- Instruct the employee what he/she is to do after the session is over. It is generally best to request that the employee leave the site immediately after having a chance to remove his/her personal belongings. You want to be somewhat flexible about the employee's departure procedure. In some instances it may be advisable to have the employee escorted off the site by a member of the security force and have his/her personal belongings sent to his/her home later. In other situations, it may be better to let the employee leave at the end of the day and permit him/her to say goodbye to his/her coworkers.

- Close the session on a positive note—lead the employee to the door and with a smile and sincere look on your face and pleasant tone of voice say something like this, "Mr. Hurtz, I wish you well and I'll try to help you in any appropriate way I can in the future."

- Return to your office and while the details of the session are fresh in your mind write up the session for documentation purposes.

- Conduct the termination session in a way that protects you and your organization from discrimination or due process violation suits. This means you need to exercise great caution in what you say and write and be prepared to justify your action by thorough documentation.

- Please note that upon the advice of their legal counsel many organizations refuse to state the reason(s) for the termination to protect themselves from being sued by the terminated employee.

TOPIC 40

Resolving Interpersonal Conflict Between Employees

"The harder the conflict, the more glorious the triumph. What we obtain too cheaply, we esteem too lightly"
—Thomas Paine

A. Things to Know

- Today's managers are spending more and more time mediating conflict between individuals and among groups.
- Our focus will be on resolving the conflict between two employees, although many of the ideas presented apply to resolving group conflict as well.
- As a manager you have two goals in your role as a mediator:
  1. To control the problem quickly so that the adverse results of the dispute are minimum for the work unit and the organization
  2. To settle the conflict in a manner considered to be fair by the involved people.

1. The Manager's Responsibilities as Mediator:

- To be perceived as impartial, fair, and trustworthy
- To be viewed as a competent mediator
- To receive training in conflict management so he/she will possess the necessary knowledge and skills for mediating effectively
- To secure all the relevant facts related to the situation and understand the positions of both parties involved
- To study the personnel folders of both antagonists to gain background information and to develop insights into the employee's job attitudes, behavior, and performance
- To have confidential talks with people who are knowledgeable about the dispute to develop perspective
- To schedule conciliation sessions at appropriate times

- To hold meetings at a private and neutral venue with comfortable seating
- To create and maintain the proper climate that encourages frank discussion by both involved people
- To identify the causes and analyze the scope and intensity of the conflict
- To gain acceptance of the ground rules for discussing the issues
- To select a strategy for settling the conflict that provides sufficient flexibility so that adjustments can be made as needed
- To primarily listen and to make timely clarifying comments as well as to ask questions that lead the discussion in the desire direction
- To explain the consequences for the disputants if they fail to reconcile their differences.

2. Recommended Attitude and Behavior of Managers Regarding Mediation:

- Strive to be objective, impartial, and act fairly
- Listen with an open mind without pre-judging or jumping to conclusions
- Insist both parties own the problem and accept the responsibility for solving the problem
- View the mediator's role as a facilitator rather than as a judge or problem solver
- Make the two antagonists responsible for solving their differences and propose the solution yourself only as a last resort
- Emphasize what is right rather than who is right
- Encourage the disputants to express their thoughts and feelings candidly and to identify options for solving the dispute
- Feel empathy and respect for both individuals
- Guide the conciliation discussion in a way that enables both employees to win and to feel that their problem has been resolved

- Discourage both people from blaming, faultfinding, name-calling, put downs, and insulting each other
- Accept the fact that some conflict is normal and inevitable and can potentially be constructive
- Desire to be helpful without taking over the problem
- Be willing to be patient, control your feelings and to hear out both employees
- Allow the employees to express their hostility and angry feelings
- Desire to identify the causes of the problem and to assist with their solution without taking over the problem
- Recognize that no strategy for resolving conflict can succeed unless the two people involved want to resolve their differences

3. Causes of Conflict:

There are two primary causes of conflict: (1) substantive and (2) emotional

1. Substantive causes:
   - Excessive work pressures in this era of "lean and mean" and demands for greater productivity
   - Authority and resources available not commensurate with employee's responsibilities and expected productivity
   - Fuzzy job descriptions or overlapping job functions
   - Struggles to protect one's power and "territory" from encroachment
   - Misunderstandings about performance goals, standards, and priorities
   - Disagreement over methods and processes for doing work
   - Different viewpoints regarding pace of work and deadlines
   - Struggle to obtain scarce resources to do job well
   - Misunderstanding over information and facts
   - Confusion and uncertainties about upcoming changes
2. Emotional causes:
   - Employee's way of doing things (for example, organized versus disorganized, fast versus slow worker, thinker versus doer)
   - Different perceptions of events and situations

- Clashing personalities
- Different beliefs, values, attitudes, and backgrounds
- Feelings of jealousy, frustration, and being mistreated
- Using superior voice tone or inflammatory language when communicating
- Judging, blaming, faultfinding, and criticizing excessively
- Perceived damage to one's status or reputation
- Feelings of anxiety and uncertainty concerning job security, promotional prospects, and changes in job assignment

4. Common Symptoms of Interpersonal Conflict:

- Inadequate cooperation, coordination, and communication
- People creating problems for fellow workers
- Initiating or engaging in smear campaigns
- Circulating of malicious rumors about employees
- Insulting and abusive remarks made frequently
- Avoiding certain people, being unavailable, or acting defensive
- Making degrading remarks about employees and the organization
- Feeling of friction or tenseness in the air
- People acting overly polite in their interactions and communicating
- Unnatural silence and lack of responsiveness
- Strained look or holding of the body
- People being easily annoyed, touchy, or irritated
- Increased aloofness or acting reserved in relationships

5. Stages of the Mediating Process

There are four stages to the mediation process: (a) preparation stage; (b) fact-finding session with two parties meeting separately; (c) conciliation session with two parties meeting together; (d) techniques to guide mediators; and (e) follow up activities

A) The preparation stage
- The way you, as mediator, handle and conflict resolution procedure is crucial to its success

- Ideally conflict should be detected as early as possible so it can be dealt with before it gets worse
- Deal with the conflict in two stages:
    1. Preliminary—the two antagonists meet separately with the mediator to explain their perception of the problem and to vent their anger and hostility
    2. Conciliatory—the parties meet together with the mediator to identify areas of agreement and disagreement and to find a mutually acceptable way to reconcile their differences
- To be effective a mediator needs to learn as much as possible about both parties to the conflict
- The mediator can secure facts in three ways: (1) examine the parties' personnel files; (2) talk with coworkers who are knowledgeable about the situation; and (3) interview the two people involved in the conflict.
- Inform the two people in conflict that you will be taking confidentially with several of their coworkers, without divulging their names to obtain their perspective regarding the problem.
- Be careful not to mistake the symptoms of the problem with the actual problem.
- Develop ground rules to guide the discussions.
- Consider the essential questions to ask to obtain the relevant facts regarding the situation.
- Information to obtain by questioning includes:
    1. How strong is the conflict?
    2. Is the conflict getting worse?
    3. What are the triggering events?
    4. How great is the impact of the conflict on the organization, the productivity of the work unit, and the coworkers morale?
    5. Is the conflict primarily a substantive or an emotional issue (or both)?
    6. When should the meeting be held to discuss the problems?
    7. How much time should be scheduled for the meetings?
    8. What is the best place to hold the meetings?
    9. What ground rules for the meetings should be set for stages 2 and 3?

      10. How can the meetings involving the coworkers be kept confidential regarding coworkers' names and the content of what they say?

- After the preparation stage is concluded, inform both parties to the conflict that they will be interviewed first separately and then together and that several of their coworkers will also be interviewed confidentially to get their input regarding the issue and situation.

B) Fact-finding and separate interviewing stage:

- Hold an impartial fact-finding session with both employees separately
- Be objective, keep an open mind, and remain calm
- Explain your role as mediator, the mediation process, and the purpose of the interviewing session
- Explain precisely how the conflict is causing problems for the organization and their coworkers without preaching or scolding
- Conduct the session with a serious and businesslike demeanor
- Acknowledge that you realize each person is upset and encourage each person to express his/her frank gut level feelings about the other person's behavior and the situation
- Emphasize the need for being frank and that it is okay for both employees to vent to you
- Ask probing questions tactfully to help you pin down the employee's perception of the facts and the real problem
- Try to determine the intensity of the feelings involved, the causes, and triggering events
- Listen carefully and when you respond to what is said do it without showing either your approval or disapproval—just listen and do your best to understand the problem and how the person perceives the issues
- Attempt to identify the employee's common interests and areas of agreement and disagreement
- Strive to discover how the antagonists view each other and why
- Show that you understand the thoughts and feelings about the situation by giving feedback that demonstrates that you grasp the essence of what each person has told you

- Inform both people engaged in the conflict that their current behavior is unacceptable and exactly why it can't be tolerated
- Point out the consequences if they continue to conduct themselves in an inappropriate manner
- Ask each person to repeat, in their own words, what the consequences will be if they don't reconcile their differences immediately
- Explain to the employees that you will be taking notes at each of the sessions to help you remember key points for the record.

C) Conciliation and joint interviewing stage:
- Explain the ground rules to follow during the discussion. Have each person show he/she understands and agrees to the ground rules
- During the stage 3 discussion, it is imperative that you remain impartial and avoid taking sides during the give and take
- Be careful not to act overly aggressive or give much advice because it is best if the employees solve their own problem
- Ask if either party has any questions before beginning the discussion
- Assist both people to see that they have common needs and goals and that your previous conversation with them indicated that they already agree on several important things
- Express confidence that employees have the ability to solve their differences for the good of all concerned.

D) Techniques to guide mediators
  1. Creating the desired climate:
     - Show respect for both people
     - Protect the egos and self-esteem of both employees
     - Allow the antagonists to have their own beliefs and ways of doing things so long as they don't interfere with getting their job done effectively or cause problems
     - Be an attentive and responsive listener
     - Prohibit the use of inflammatory or insulting language
     - Choose a seating arrangement that promotes good communication and interaction between the involved employees. The chairs should be comfortable and of the

same kind and height. The chairs should be positioned semi-facing toward each other with nothing between them except for the mediator who should be seated opposite the two parties and midway between them

- Begin by discussing the issues that can be resolved quickly to get off with a positive start
- Try to get the two people to agree in principle on those things they can immediately agree to
- Encourage the employees to describe how they feel about something about the other person rather than judging the actions as good-bad or right-wrong
- Establish a low stress climate that emphasizes cooperation toward a common goal conciliation
- Focus the discussion on differences in thinking and behavior instead of personality traits (state when the discussion is making progress and when it is becoming counterproductive)
- Provide a face-saving procedure toward the end of the session if one of the people appears to be the loser in the dispute (your goal is to have both parties feel like winners)

2. Securing agreement on the nature and causes of problem(s)
   - Ask each person, in separate discussions, to explain their views about the crux of the problem(s)
   - Ask the parties to identify what they believe are the causes of the problem
   - State your perception of the problem(s) after listening to both employees' assessment of the problem and its causes
   - You and the two employees discuss the problem(s) and agree to them. Define the problem and causes in clear and specific terms. Write down the definition of the problem and the agreed upon causes so everyone involved can refer to it as needed
   - Identify and discuss and agree on the relevant facts pertaining to the situation
   - Differentiate among facts, opinions, inferences, perceptions, and feelings when discussing the matter

- Avoid discussing the solution(s) to the problem until the problem is adequately defined, the facts agreed to, and the causes identified.

3. Methods for Achieving Understanding:

- Insist each person talk directly to the other person, rather than through you, and that they respond to each other's comments and questions
- Encourage dialogue, with mutual give and take, and discourage two monologues
- Prohibit the parties from trying to refute the other person's ideas or statements until he/she has heard the other person out and shows that he/she understands what was said (for example, by accurately rephrasing what was said)
- Encourage each person to take responsibility for their own statements by using the word I consistently when stating their own thoughts and feelings
- Require that both employees speak in specifics rather than generalities
- Listen carefully to both employees to understand their thoughts, feelings, assumptions, and assertions
- Ensure that key points are heard and responded to at the opportune times by clarifying, rephrasing, and summing up what was said (especially if the statements are of a positive and conciliatory nature)
- Respond to the employee's comments by saying "I understand." Never react by saying things like "I agree with you" or "you are absolutely right" (avoid being judgmental)
- Use language that is soothing, supportive, unifying, and that reduces tension
- Ask for feedback periodically to verify that the parties understand each other (for example, "Ley, what do you think about what Jack just said?")
- Require that both people listen attentively without interrupting each other except to clarify something just said
- Emphasize that the important thing is what is right not who is right

- Discourage the two people from being closed-minded and holding rigid inflexible positions that are divisive.

4. Ways to Solve a Problem

- The goal of the conciliation stage is to find a fair and mutually acceptable solution to the conflict as opposed to an expedient one that could actually make the situation worse
- Delay any discussion of possible solutions to the conflict until all the pertinent facts are known and all causes of the problem are identified and agreed upon
- Discover as many viable options as the mediator and two conflicting people can to improve the chances of finding an acceptable solution
- Discourage either person from getting into a firm proposed solution before exploring all alternatives
- Be imaginative when searching for an acceptable solution. If you are encountering difficulty coming up with a satisfactory solution, it is worth entering a "fantasy world" where you can speculate and discuss imaginative solutions such as "suppose we were to . . ." or "what would happen if we were to. . . .?"
- Ask each person to suggest a fair solution. One way of doing this is to have each person write her/his solution separately on a piece of paper and give each proposal to the mediator to read and then be discussed by all those involved
- Seek a compromise on a solution when the discussion fails to result in a mutually agreeable solution (a compromise is a reasonable approach for breaking an impasse, no one wins and no one loses)
- Remind the two employees that there is a deadline for the reconciliation to occur and state the consequences if an acceptable solution can't be reached
- When a solution is agreed to, have the two parties explain their understanding of the agreed upon solution
- The agreement should reduce the tension and help both people to work together cooperatively, amiably, and productively

- Next, discuss how best to implement the solution agreed to
- The mediator should make sure that any relevant organizational policies/procedures and or union contract provisions are followed
- Offer to assist the people to make the necessary adjustments.

E. The follow-up activities

- As soon as the solution is agreed to, give a copy of the conciliation agreement to both parties so they can refer to it in the future as needed
- Schedule a follow-up session a week or so after the agreement became effective to determine how the people are getting along and to determine if there are any remaining problems to address
- It is a good idea to check on the progress (and level of cooperation) again a month after the agreement became effective

TOPIC 41

Conducting a Successful News Conference

"In the case of news we should always wait for the sacrament of confirmation"

—Voltaire

A. Things to Know

1. If your organization does not employ a Communications Director who would handle all press conferences, you could be asked to handle that responsibility. Therefore, it's important that you learn some of the "do's and don'ts" of holding a news conference.

   - "Press" or "News" conference are labels used interchangeably when naming this event.

   - Press conferences are held sparingly and used to inform the public and important constituents of an extraordinary happening that will impact your organization and the community in which it resides. The impact may be of a positive or a negative nature. It could also be used to react to an announcement or actions of another organization or Government.

   - Organizational news may include such topics as change in ownership or top management personnel, expansion of your organization or downsizing and loss of jobs at your organization, ground breaking for a new building, or planned diversification that will bring new business to your community.

   - Press conferences have to be newsworthy. The reason for the press conference has to be important enough to attract the media in your area and justify their sending reporters with microphones and cameras to the event.

   - Good press relations must be initiated and maintained if your organization wants to be visible in your community beyond.

- Make friends with and have contacts at local radio and television News Directors and the Editors of newspapers and news magazines. You need to know someone in the media you can trust and who also trusts you.
- If your organization decides that a press conference is the best means of informing others, it's imperative that everyone in the organization is made aware of this fact and what role each will have, even if it's just being present at the conference

2. There are many positive aspects of a well-planned and conducted news conference. These include:
   - A press conference is by its very nature, free advertising for your organization.
   - The presence of the media actually makes the announcement or event even more newsworthy.
   - A press conference can disseminate more information than a printed news release or phone interview and do it one time for all media outlets.
   - It is interactive with questions from the media and answers from the organization's spokespeople.
   - It can be an opportune time to halt rumors and contradict any other negative information that may be circulating in the community.
   - A press conference will be a morale booster for your organization. From top management down, most employees will feel proud of their organization and be pleased they were in the news.

B. Things to Do

1. Careful planning with attention to detail is critical if a news conference is to be successful. This is an organizational event to which the media have been invited and lasting impressions of the organization and its personnel will be made. There are many things to do to ensure success:
   - Start planning early. A week or 2 weeks is recommended.
   - Discuss the press conference with top management and determine the purpose and focus of the conference.
   - Decide who will be part of the group planning the event. This should include one or more from the executive level.

- Decide who will be the spokesperson or moderator of the press conference. This person has to be part of the planning group.
- If needed, compile a comprehensive list of media in your area with names and contact information for Assignment Editors and News Directors and others in the media you may have worked with before.
- Invite the media as soon as possible and in collaboration with the media contacts select the best time, date, and location for the conference. Note- without the media in attendance, you have no news conference.
- Mail out a press release or news advisory with all pertinent information about the event that includes any historical background and all major participants.
- Design a Press Kit to give to reporters the day of the conference or mail it in advance to help them better prepare.
- The Press Kit should contain: list of conference participants with short biographies and photos if possible, a copy of Press Release stating organization's position on an issue or the activity the organization is or will be conducting, pertinent historical information that has meaning for the conference focus, other photos of organization's people or place, and any other press releases from your organization or its subsidiaries.
- Prepare scripts for the persons speaking and the order in which they will speak. Ask them to practice and work for clarity of subject using good public speaking techniques. Tell them there will be a "run through" practice prior to the public event.
- Prepare the meeting room or off site location. If this is a "ground breaking" it is preferable to hold the information session indoors near the site and then move outdoors for the actual ground breaking. Weather could play an important part in any outside activities.
- For press conferences inside or out, you must provide AC power for the organization's microphones and loudspeakers and also for the news reporters if necessary (most reporters attend with battery-powered cameras and recorders).

- As a courtesy, seating should be provided for the reporters with room for their equipment. In many cases, the TV photojournalist is also a reporter and is busy with equipment. Radio and print reporters often choose to sit down to listen and take notes or record audio.
- There needs to be a podium set up at the front of the room for the moderator and other speaking participants that has a microphone and necessary lighting. Bottled water should be available for all speakers near the podium.
- As the day approaches get all speakers together and actually conduct a "dry run." You will coach them through the process and act as a reporter when it is time for the question and answer period.
- Top management people should decide who is going to greet and attend to any dignitaries who will be attending but not taking part. Decide if they warrant their own sitting area and/or introduction to those gathered.
- If there is a stage or dais, the list of who is attending and who should be sitting on the dais needs to be decided early on in the planning.
- The day of the event you must make the members of the media your sole focus.
- Welcome media representatives to the press conference personally as they arrive. Ask them to sign in and show them the general area that is designated for the press. Encourage them to seek you out if they need anything before, during, or after the conference.
- Seat the conference participants in the predetermined location. This could be seats on the dais or in a semicircle to either side of the podium.
- The conference coordinator should give the moderator the signal to begin and let him/her welcome the press first, visiting dignitaries next, and then the general population that is attending.
- The moderator then introduces the participants with a speaking role and invites the first speaker (often the President or CEO of

the organization) to the podium to give his/her presentation and begin the press conference in earnest.

- Things to remember: Press conferences work best if brief, factual, and on task. No more than 3 to 5 minutes for each speaker.
- The moderator should then field the questions from the reporters and pass the question on to the appropriate participant to respond.
- Q & A can last until all questions have been asked and answered but no more than a maximum of 45 minutes. Reporters have other stories to cover elsewhere and have to have all the information back to the station or press room to meet their deadlines.
- The moderator thanks the press (and others) for attending and if appropriate invites all to stay for light refreshments. You should try to touch base with each reporter if possible and thank them for coming and that you'll look forward to seeing, reading, or listening to their report.
- Be sure to check in with the CEO to get his/her reaction to the conference and to thank him/her for participating.
- Within the next day or two, meet with those who organized the Press Conference and debrief. Examine what went well, what could have been done better, and how to fix it. Follow up with members of the media that you have a relationship with and ask for their feedback. Then put it all to bed until the next opportunity comes along for another conference.

TOPIC 42

Testifying Competently in Public Hearings

"Communicate to express—not to impress"

—Unknown

A. Things to Know

Preparing to testify:

1. Collecting Information:

- Secure important information about the hearing group well in advance of the hearing date
- Find out the purpose of the hearing and specifically why the group wants to hear you testify
- Become informed about the typical hearing procedures and methods (the ground rules)
- Consult with these sources to obtain valuable information about how to present effective testimony:
  1. Your professional or trade association
  2. Public relations firms and consultants
  3. People experienced in giving testimony such as attorneys and expert witnesses
  4. Read books and articles on how to provide competent testimony
  5. Watch public hearings on television (for example, congressional hearings) and observe how the witnesses render testimony
- Predict questions you may be asked and prepare answers to these questions before the hearing
- Visit the hearing room ahead of time to get familiar with it

2. Organizing Your Information:

- Prepare your notes in an organized manner
- Type the subject line in capital letters and double space all the information

- Highlight all key points
- Number all pages in the upper right-hand corner of your note cards or paper
- List all subjects alphabetically or by type of subject and have a system for locating each subject quickly
- Have duplicate information available if needed

3. Selecting Your Support Staff for the Hearing

- Refrain from appearing in the hearing without adequate support staff. The number and type will be contingent upon the complexity of the subject. However, it is usually advisable to have at least legal counsel and an expert on the subject present as back up.
- Feel free to consult with members of your support team whenever you need assistance. However, it is best not to rely on your back-up people too much or if may affect your own credibility.
- Figure out the best seating positions for your support staff. You need to be able to confer with your advisors quickly when you need to without appearing to be overly dependent on them.
- Two positions for support staff seating are frequently used:
  1. Sitting close behind you, slightly to the left or right of you, so you can see and confer with each other quickly and without being overheard.
  2. Sitting alongside of you. This position aids communicating with each other, but can make it appear that you are overly reliant on them throughout the proceedings.

4. Rehearse Your Presentation:

- You need to rehearse two things when preparing to testify at a public hearing:
  1. Your opening remarks
  2. Answers to anticipated questions from members of the hearing body.
- Practice your opening remarks enough so you can maintain eye contact with the entire hearing body.
- Strive to speak from brief notes in an extemporaneous manner. Avoid either memorizing or reading your comments.

- When answering a member's question look at him/her briefly at the start of your answer and then focus on all the hearing members.

B. Things to Do

1. Preliminary Activities:

- Place all your notes and reference material where they can be referred to quickly
- Seat your back-up people strategically
- Keep a cool glass (or bottles) of water close by
- Test the microphone to ensure it is at the right height for you, is loud enough, and that it doesn't have an irritating screeching sound
- Acknowledge the presence of hearing members with a nod and brief smile

2. Presentation Style:

- Give a brief relevant and impressive opening statement. Maintain eye contact when making your comments and offer them without reading them as much as possible.
- Act natural and project integrity, sincerity, and competency
- Act poised and confident, not arrogant or condescending
- Sit at the witness table alertly without any hint of anxiety or defiance
- Speak from memory as much as possible and use your notes minimally to show you are on top of things
- Speak confidently with a pleasant voice tone loud enough to be heard easily; avoid dropping your voice volume or increasing your pitch level at the end of sentences
- Speak at a measured pace and pause for affect at appropriate times
- Pronounce your words carefully. Speak with wide open mouth and move your lips freely to help you enunciate clearly
- Avoid mumbling and keep your mouth empty of food and chewing gum
- Be brief and avoid long drawn-out comments when addressing the group or answering questions

- Balance conciseness and the need to be complete when providing information
- Act open and cooperative rather than combative and defensive
- Act calm and composed when speaking and listening to group members
- Try not to act tired or irritated so that you don't appear to be vulnerable
- Listen politely and attentively to all comments and questions of hearing members
- Explain all technical terms or complicated concepts as simply as possible without sounding as though you were talking down to the group

3. Answering Questions Competently:

- Ask if you can make an opening statement before answering any questions
- Be patient and polite and avoid antagonizing your questioners
- Answer all questions candidly and cooperatively—don't act reluctant or evasive and avoid making contradictory or inconsistent statements and answers
- Refrain from guessing or bluffing with your answers
- Say "I don't know" to a question if it is the truth. Volunteer to find the answer and provide it later.
- Protect your credibility by never giving evasive responses such as these: "I guess that is possible" or "I may have said that I don't remember"
- Politely but firmly refuse to answer speculative questions
- When asked repetitive questions politely point out you have answered the question before
- When accused of giving contradictory answers simply state "I don't concur with that statement"
- Avoid being intimidated by a series of rapid questions
- When answering an important question try your best to complete your answer despite the efforts of the questioner to interrupt you
- Insist on using your own words and don't allow questioners to put words in your mouth

- Rephrase loaded or leading questions before answering them
- Look at all questioners with the same degree of interest, body positioning, and facial expressions regardless of whether the question is of a friendly or hostile type.

4. Watch Your Body Language:

- Be aware of what your body language is conveying as you are talking—be equally alert to what your questioner's body is signaling to you as he/she listens to your responses to questions
- Avoid looking anxious or uptight when answering tough questions that the questioner is responding negatively to
- Be aware of any nervous mannerisms that your body is sending such as: playing with your pen, touching jewelry, rubbing your head or looking down or away while speaking or answering question.

5. Cautions to Observe:

- Be sure your notes and records are organized so that you can refer to them quickly when needed
- Take notes when a long winded questioner is asking several questions at once so you can remember and respond to them
- When you can't recall information that you are asked about, ask for time to locate the information in your records
- Be careful not to interrupt members asking you questions and never abruptly contradict what they are saying—you want to avoid embarrassing any hearing member
- Ask for any unclear questions to be clarified before answering the questions
- Ask for time to examine any unfamiliar documents before commenting on them
- Take the time to digest unpredicted, complicated, or touchy questions
- Always assume the microphone is turned on and act accordingly. Block the microphone with your hand and avoid talking into it when conferring with your aides
- Try not to rely on your advisors too much

TOPIC 43

Speaking Before a Hostile Group

"It is often better not to see an insult than to avenge it"

—Seneca

A. Things to Know

1. There are occasions when, as a manager, you will find yourself in front of an audience that does not agree with your organization's policies or actions. They truly believe it will adversely affect their lives. This can also hold true for certain decisions that you make or actions that you take as a manager.

    • As the spokesperson for the organization, you become the focus of the group's hostility.

    • You need to be prepared to cope with two sources of hostility (1) that which is based on people having the facts and understanding your views and are angry about it; (2) that which is based on lack of understanding and faulty facts.

    • You must do your homework to be exceptionally well prepared with accurate information and honest answers.

    • Your hope is that by stating your ideas clearly and backed by facts and sound reasons the audience will become less hostile and more receptive to your ideas and views.

    • There are ways to help diffuse a hostile audience that all managers should be mindful of practice before a confrontational discussion or presentation is held.

    • Accept the fact that the hostile members of the audience feel their viewpoints are just as logical as yours.

    • The art of dealing with a hostile audience or group is challenging for any manager and requires special skills and careful handling.

B. Things to Do

1. Key recommendations include:

    - Arrive early and engage in "small talk" with people who you know understand the issues. Let others see you chatting, smiling, or even laughing with these coworkers.
    - On a stage or at floor level sit confidently and in a relaxed manner prior to and during the introduction.
    - Approach the podium with assurance but without cockiness, and above all, without any hint of belligerence.
    - Before you speak, ask the moderator to request the opposition to be fair to the speaker(s) and to others in the audience (on occasions when you know the audience disagrees with your viewpoints).
    - In your opening remarks greet the audience making eye contact and express your appreciation for being invited to talk and share your views about the subject.
    - Pledge to present all sides of the issue in a fair and balanced manner.
    - Commend the American Way that gives people the right to express their ideas freely and to disagree without being disagreeable.
    - Commend the opposing viewpoint on something that is accepted as being important to the audience and that you can ethically agree with.
    - Have a friendly and pleasant look on your face and speak without any hint of belligerency in your voice.
    - Restrict your opening remarks to reviewing the important points of agreement between you and the audience. Use terminology compatible with your listener's vocabulary and background if possible.
    - Lower your voice deliberately and resist the temptation to raise it when addressing a noisy crowd.
    - Ignore hecklers and never personalize your comments to a hostile audience. Keep your remarks strictly impersonal and objective. Avoid doing anything to inflame or insult people as this solidifies opposition.

- If there is a question and answer period, all questions from the audience should be written and turned into the chairperson to screen and if appropriate to pass on to you. Oral questions should be avoided to prevent negative remarks or "speech making" by members of the audience trying to upset the decorum.

2. If the audience is excessively noisy, these approaches are recommended:
   - Sit quietly for a few minutes with the hope the noise will end soon and have the chairperson ask audience to cooperate by settling down and being quiet.
   - Simply end the talk. Communication is over anyhow.
   - Have security remove the hecklers if there are only a few causing the disruption.
   - Invite a member of the opposition to the podium and permit him/her to speak first, without interruption, for a specific period of time (this might also be planned ahead of time).
   - Be sure to have the dissident speaker reciprocate by listening attentively and politely to the scheduled speaker. Next give your intended speech without any reference to the opposition's remarks whatsoever.

3. If part of your presentation is to persuade the audience to see the necessity of a policy or corporate action or to see it differently, use these five steps to make your case:
   - Identify cause of hostility
   - Pick out something from the opposing viewpoint you can agree with
   - Show you understand their objections
   - Demonstrate the merits of your case
   - Have a strong conclusion with a succinct summary of your arguments.

Preventing and Controlling Malicious Rumors

"In times of calamity any rumor is believed"
—Rubilius Syrus

A. Things to Know

1. Nature of Rumors:

- A rumor is a report or account of some incident, situation, decision, or action that has no known source. The information that is circulating is unauthorized and unverified.
- Rumors are spread by a system known as the grapevine.
- Rumors will always exist. They are a fact of life for all organizations. It is unrealistic for managers to expect that rumors will ever cease because they exist to fill a basic need to employees to obtain information that doesn't come to them from any official source.
- A manager's goal is to reduce the number of rumors by offering prompt, complete, and current information on matters of interest to employees.
- Rumors are typically true to some extent, although the details are frequently incorrect.
- Most minor rumors are harmless and will either be ignored or die a natural death.
- The effect of rumors ranges from the annoying, or in the case of malicious rumors extremely harmful (note: bull sessions or shop talk regularly take place at work and can often be helpful rather than harmful. For example, they give employees a chance to let off steam).
- Rumors travel with astounding speed and it is difficult to stop them. Therefore, it is imperative that managers move quickly

to employ countermeasures to minimize or contain them to limit their impact.

- Rumors develop and grow in direct proportion to their importance to people and reflect the biases of the people circulating them.
- It is difficult, if not impossible, to track down the exact source of a rumor because a rumor usually involves several people.
- It is wise to have the most credible and trusted managers assigned to refute the rumor by supplying the correct information and to answer questions. In the event the managers don't know the answers to the employee questions, they should state frankly that they don't know the answer, but will find out the answer and share it by a specific date.
- It is essential for managers attempting to refute the rumor to not repeat the wording of the rumor because repeating it verbatim would only reinforce the rumor in the minds of the employee (the more a rumor is repeated the more believable it becomes).
- When employees receive a message from both the official channels and the grapevine, they frequently believe the grapevine more.
- Managers should strive to understand how the grapevine works and use it to their benefit instead of trying to destroy it completely (for example, managers could use it as a part of their pipeline).

2. Causes of Rumors

- Prolonged delays in making decisions and taking action on important matters cause rumors
- Official channels often transmit incomplete information and do it too slowly
- Organizational conflict and antagonism among employees is widespread
- Serious problems exist that are ignored by management

- Erroneous information is circulated frequently and creates speculation
- Feelings of anxiety and job insecurity are prevalent among the employees
- Employees feel powerless and that they have no control over their working conditions and future
- Management fails to give communicating with employees a top priority and consequently needed information is lacking.

B. Things to Do

1. Methods for Discouraging Rumors:

- Management proactively learning what kind of information employees want and need and their preferred sources and methods for receiving it
- Managers maintaining an open-door policy and going out into the employee work areas and workstations to find out how things are going and what is on employee's mind
- Managers sharing the organization's policies and procedures regarding rumors at the new employee orientation sessions and in the employee handbook
- Managers keeping official channels open and unclogged so information can flow quickly in all directions
- Organizational policy requires that managers keep their employees fully informed
- Maintain manager pipelines that keep managers alerted to employee problems and dissatisfaction
- Managers actively promote a healthy communications climate
- Management shares both good and bad news with employees
- Management is trusted by employees and has a reputation for fair and ethical treatment of employees
- Management provides employees important information in advance and especially regarding deadlines, target dates, and changes

- Management keeps information labeled as confidential to the minimum because secretiveness breeds suspicion and anxiety
- Management uses a variety of communications methods to keep employees informed
- Management explains its reasons for decisions and actions routinely, candidly, and in a timely fashion
- Employees feel adequately informed on all important matters including their work duties, job security, opportunities for raises and promotion (employees know where they stand and how they are doing)
- The organization employs a full-time Director of Communications to coordinate all communications activities

2. Coping with a Circulating Rumor:

- Gather all the relevant data pertaining to the rumor quickly and analyze the scope, seriousness, and impact of the rumor before doing anything
- Decide whether it is best to take corrective action or merely ignore the rumor with the hope it will quickly die on its own
- Identify the possible courses of action for the type of rumor
- Hold a planning meeting with the organization's director of communications and communications advisory council
- Meet with the organization's official and unofficial leaders to discuss the situation and solicit their assistance in spreading the correct information informally
- Determine the specific causes, possible motives, originators, and main disseminators of the rumor
- Prepare an authoritative, complete, and candid announcement explaining the real situation without mentioning the rumor itself (you don't want to reinforce the rumor by repeating it)
- Combat malicious destructive rumors by using multiple methods which could include the following to inform the employees of the actual facts and situation:
  1. Post a clarifying announcement on all of the organization's locked bulletin boards. The information should include how to

gain additional information by calling the organization's telephone hotline.

2. Check to see that the hotline is working and that the message is brief, clear, and audible.

3. Send e-mails to immediately transmit the correct information.

4. Have trusted employees feed the grapevine with the accurate information.

5. Conduct face-to-face grassroots meetings with employees to answer their questions.

6. Hold face-to-face supportive sessions with employees or departments being harmed by a malicious rumor to reassure them and minimize their anxiety.

7. Discipline the employee who originated the rumor in a severe manner and spell out the consequences if the action is ever repeated (the discipline could be getting fired).

8. Discipline the employees who were the most active in spreading the rumor and warn them of the consequences of a repeat offense.

- Remind all employees of the organization's policies and procedures regarding rumors. Also remind them of how to report rumors and of the consequences of being involved with the spreading of malicious rumors.

- Hold a clarifying news conference if the rumor is creating problems in the community or damaging the organization's reputation in their industry.

8 COMPONENTS OF THE COMMUNICATIONS PROCESS

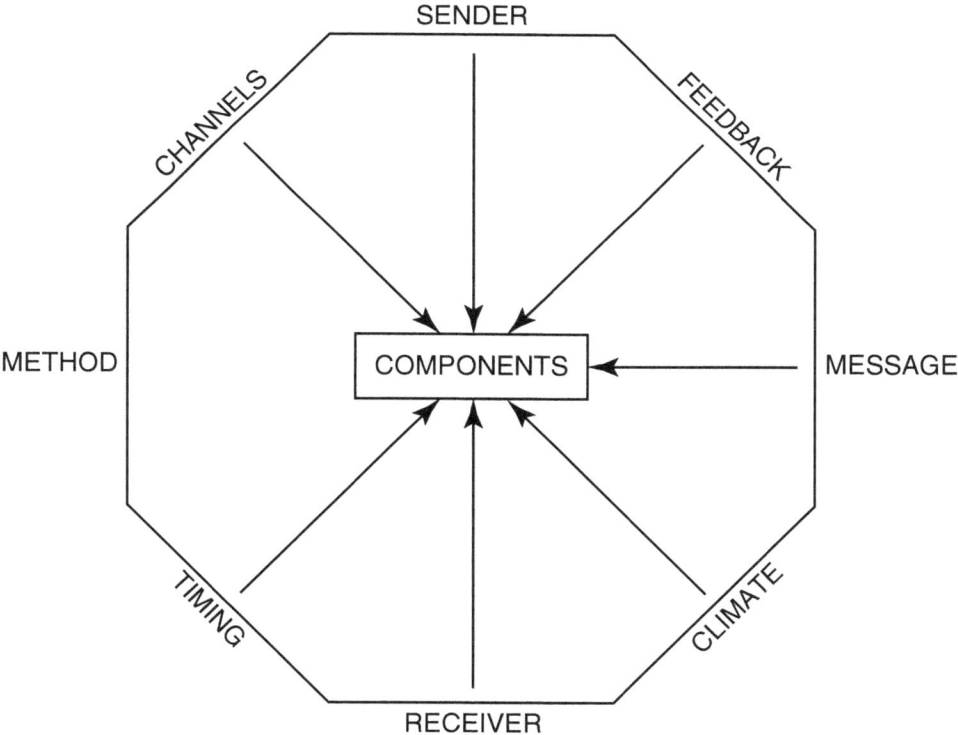

Index

OTHER TITLES IN OUR CORPORATE COMMUNICATION COLLECTION

Debbie DuFrene, Stephen F. Austin State University, *Editor*

- *Managerial Communication for the Arabian Gulf* by Valerie Priscilla Goby, Catherine Nickerson, and Chrysi Rapanta
- *Managerial Communication* by Reginald L. Bell and Jeanette S. Martin
- *Writing for the Workplace: Business Communication for Professionals* by Janet Mizrahi
- *Get Along, Get It Done, Get Ahead: Interpersonal Communication in the Diverse Workplace* by Geraldine E. Hynes
- *Managing Virtual Teams, Second Edition* by Debbie D. DuFrene and Carol M. Lehman
- *The Language of Success: The Confidence and Ability to Say What You Mean and Mean What You Say in Business and Life* by Kim Wilkerson and Alan Weiss
- *Writing Online: A Guide To Effective Digital Communication at Work* by Erika Darics
- *Writing For Public Relations: A Practical Guide for Professionals* by Janet Mizrahi
- *Technical Marketing Communication: A Guide to Writing, Design, and Delivery* by Emil B. Towner and Heidi L. Everett
- *Communication for Consultants* by Rita R. Owens
- *Planning and Organizing Business Reports: Written, Oral, and Research-Based* by Dorinda Clippinger
- *Zen and the Art of Business Communication: A Step-by-Step Guide to Improving Your Business Writing Skills* by Susan L. Luck
- *The Essential Guide to Business Communication for Finance Professionals* by Jason L. Snyder and Lisa A.C. Frank
- *Essential Communications Skills for Managers, Volume II: A Practical Guide for Communicating Effectively with All People in All Situations* by Walter St. John and Ben Haskell

Announcing the Business Expert Press Digital Library

Concise e-books business students need for classroom and research

This book can also be purchased in an e-book collection by your library as

- *a one-time purchase,*
- *that is owned forever,*
- *allows for simultaneous readers,*
- *has no restrictions on printing, and*
- *can be downloaded as PDFs from within the library community.*

Our digital library collections are a great solution to beat the rising cost of textbooks. E-books can be loaded into their course management systems or onto students' e-book readers. The **Business Expert Press** digital libraries are very affordable, with no obligation to buy in future years. For more information, please visit **www.businessexpertpress.com/librarians**. To set up a trial in the United States, please email **sales@businessexpertpress.com**

www.ingramcontent.com/pod-product-compliance
Lightning Source LLC
Chambersburg PA
CBHW071632200326
41519CB00012BA/2264